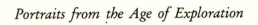

*Portraits from the Age of Exploration*

# PORTRAITS FROM THE AGE OF EXPLORATION

Selections from André Thevet's
*Les vrais pourtraits et vies
des hommes illustres*

EDITED BY
*Roger Schlesinger*

TRANSLATED BY
*Edward Benson*

UNIVERSITY OF ILLINOIS PRESS
*Urbana and Chicago*

Library of Congress Cataloging-in-Publication Data

Thevet, André, 1502–1590.
    [Vrais pourtraits et vies des hommes illustres.   English.
Selections]
    Portraits from the age of exploration : selections from André
Thevet's Les vrais pourtraits et vies des hommes illustres / edited
by Roger Schlesinger ; translated by Edward Benson.
       p.   cm.
    Includes bibliographical references and index.
    ISBN 0-252-01943-1 (cl : alk. paper)
    1. Biography—Dictionaries—Early works to 1800.   I. Schlesinger,
Roger, 1943– .  II. Title.
CT102.T48   1993
920.02–dc20
   [B]                                      91–46218
                                               CIP

R. S.: For Steve, my brother

E. B.: For Kate

# Contents

# Acknowledgments

Edward Benson wishes to thank the dean of arts and sciences at Central Missouri State University for his support.

Roger Schlesinger wishes to express appreciation to the Newberry Library for a Columbian Quincentennial Fellowship, which got this project off to a good start, and Washington State University for a professional leave with which to complete it. Special thanks are due to several individuals at Washington State University: Richard Hume, the head of the history department, for his enthusiastic support; Thomas Faulkner for preparing the camera-ready copy for this book at the Humanities Research Center; and Mary Watrous for computer expertise and sensible advice.

Both wish to thank their editors, Elizabeth G. Dulany and Mary Giles at the University of Illinois Press and Rachele Duke at the University of New Mexico, who translated the epitaphs in the chapters on Columbus and Vespucci from Italian and Latin respectively, and the epitaph in the Cortés chapter (note 21) from Italian. All illustrations are from Thevet's *Les vrais pourtraits et vies des hommes illustres* (1584) and *Cosmographie universelle* (1575) and are used through the courtesy of the Newberry Library.

PORTRAITS FROM THE AGE OF EXPLORATION

# Introduction

Published for the first time in 1584, André Thevet's *Les vrais pourtraits et vies des hommes illustres* is outstanding among Renaissance collections of biographies because of its great variety of subjects.[1] It encompasses more than two hundred lives, drawn from virtually all regions of the world, from antiquity to Thevet's own sixteenth century, and it contains the first biographies in European literature of Native Americans. These six chapters, together with another six describing the lives of prominent European explorers, help to illuminate the European mentality as it encountered strange and exotic peoples.

*Vrais pourtraits*, however, is more than simply a collection of biographical data. It also sheds light on Thevet's own *mentalité*; understanding it, therefore, is vital for a balanced assessment of Thevet and his work. Here, in his last published book, he most clearly reveals himself as an enthusiastic supporter of monarchy and Roman Catholicism. As a court favorite who eventually enjoyed the patronage of four French kings, Thevet strongly supported the idea of monarchy and personal rule in both European and American societies. Janet Whatley's assertion that his judgments "are profoundly reassuring to the authorities in place"[2] is certainly true of *Vrais pourtraits*. In addition, he described the proselytizing activities of the Church in most favorable terms, and even defended Spanish treatment of American Indians. He also argued passionately against his Huguenot adversaries, especially the Calvinist minister Jean de Léry.

1. Cf., for example, the more limited scope of other contemporary collections: Paolo Giovio, *Elogia veris clarorum virorum* (Venice, 1546); Georgio Vasari, *Le vite de piu eccellenti architetti, pittori, et scultori italiani* (Florence, 1550; 2d ed., 1568); and Antoine du Verdier, *La biographie, et prosopographie des roys de France* (Paris, 1583).

2. Whatley, "Savage Hierarchies," 324.

Thevet's assessment of America and its inhabitants, moreover, reveals his ambivalence about the New World. On the one hand, he firmly believed in the innate superiority of European values and institutions and in the righteousness of the European conquest of the Indians. At the same time, he obviously respected and admired some New World rulers and considered some facets of their societies to be equal or even superior to their European equivalents. In addition, Thevet intended his biographies of these illustrious and exotic New World figures to do more than merely satisfy the curiosity of his readers; they would show that the lessons he wished to illustrate were valid for parts of the world beyond the confines of Europe.

# Thevet's Life and Works

Historians know little about Thevet's life.[1] He was born in An-goulême, but even the date of his birth is uncertain. Until recently, scholars believed that the correct dates for his life were 1502–90 or, more likely, 1504–92, but Frank Lestringant, on the basis of an un-equivocal statement by Thevet himself,[2] makes a convincing case for a birthdate of 1516 or 1517. Later, with the support of the powerful La Rochefoucauld family, he obtained a university education at Poitiers and Paris and then secured an appointment as private secretary to the Cardinal of Amboise. Perhaps inspired by the books in the cardinal's library at Gaillon, Thevet developed a strong interest in travel and made several journeys to Italy, Switzerland, Naples, and Africa in the 1540s. Indeed, he eventually became one of the most widely traveled Frenchmen of his day and claimed to have spent seventeen years in foreign places.[3]

Thevet's career as an author of geographical literature began with a journey to the Middle East. In June 1549, under the patronage of the Cardinal of Lorraine, he sailed from Venice to the Levant, where he remained for four years. During this period he toured Constantinople with the Genoese ambassador in November 1549 and accompanied the celebrated naturalist Pierre Gilles to Chalcedonia, Rhodes, Athens, and Alexandria in a search for antiquities in 1550. He also visited Lebanon, Arabia, and Malta before returning home.[4]

1. The information presented herein is essentially the same as that which appears in the Introduction of *André Thevet's North America*, ed. Schlesinger and trans. Stabler; additional translations from the French are by Edward Benson.

2. André Thevet, *Cosmographie de Levant*, ed. Frank Lestringant (Geneva, 1985), xiii.

3. Thevet, *Cosmographie universelle*, 1:Dedication.

4. Louis Moréri, *Le grand dictionnaire historique* (Paris, 1759), 10:138.

In 1554, he published an account of his travels in the East under the title *Cosmographie de Levant*, which he dedicated to his former patron, François de la Rochefoucauld.

Thevet capitalized on the success of his first book by seizing an opportunity to travel to the New World, and in so doing became an author of even greater reputation. In 1555, he obtained the position of *aumonier* (chaplain) for the expedition to Brazil of Nicholas Durand, chevalier de Villegaignon. Thevet landed at Guanabara (Rio de Janeiro) on 10 November 1555 but fell ill soon thereafter and returned to France on the first available ship about ten weeks later. Upon his arrival there he published his second work, *Les singularitez de la France Antarctique, autrement nommée Amerique: & de plusieurs terres & isles decouvertes de nostre temps* (Paris, 1557). Here, in the first illustrated French book about the New World, Thevet discussed the fate of the Villegaignon expedition, contributed valuable ethnographic data on the customs of the Tupinamba Indians, and gave exact descriptions of animals and plants. He also included accounts of Mexico, Florida, and Canada, regions that he claimed to have visited on the return journey to France. Frank Lestringant, the best-known authority on Thevet, concluded that *Singularitez* is "without question a seminal work for sixteenth century travel literature. With this work, devoted in large measure to Native American cannibals of the Rio de Janeiro area, a current appears which will continue in the works of Léry, then Montaigne, to culminate finally in the Age of Enlightenment in the myth of the Noble Savage so dear to Diderot and Raynal."[5] His more recent assessment of Thevet's work is that "we consider him one of the very first of the modern ethnographers."[6]

Lestringant's opinion echoed Thevet's contemporaries, who also gave *Singularitez* a favorable reception. French editions appeared in Paris and Antwerp in 1558, and in 1561 and 1568 Italian and English translations were published in Venice and London respectively. As a

5. Frank Lestingrant, ed., *Les Singularités de la France Antarctique. Le Brésil des cannibales au xvie siècle* (Paris, 1983), 7.

6. Frank Lestringant, "L'insulaire de Rabelais, ou la fiction en archipel (Pour une lecture topographique du 'quart livre')," in *Rabelais en son demi-millénaire: Actes du colloque international de Tours (24–29 Septembre, 1984)*, ed. Jean Céard and Jean-Claude Margolin, in *Etudes Rabelaisiennes 21, Travaux d'Humanisme et Renaissance 225* (Geneva, 1988), 253.

result of his two successful geographical accounts, Thevet obtained a number of positions at court and in the church. He became *aumonier* to Catherine de Medici, royal cosmographer (royal geographer) to four French kings beginning with Henri II, canon of the Cathedral in Angoulême, abbot of Notre Dame of Madion in Saintonge, and overseer of the Royal Collection of Curiosities at Fontainebleau.

Although Thevet made no journeys to the New World after publication of *Singularitez*, he did write several additional travel accounts, including, in 1575, his most extensive work, *La Cosmographie universelle d'André Thevet, cosmographe du roy*. The Brazilian section of this book is more complete than *Singularitez*, and is important for its description of the style of life and beliefs of the Tupinamba. Indeed, the account of these Indians is among the best extant, based on the author's own experiences and perhaps on interviews with others. However, Thevet also attempted to convey an entirely different impression of his voyage to the New World, especially to North America, than he had presented in *Singularitez*.[7] In the earlier work he wrote that he had been "very close to Canada" but now—almost twenty years later—he asserted that he landed there and spent more than twenty days examining the country. In fact, Thevet wrote his descriptions of Canada in *Cosmographie* as if he were recounting his own personal experiences, and he even included accounts of conversations with natives.[8]

Understandably, the publication of *Cosmographie* began the decline of Thevet's reputation as a scholar. Jean de Léry, one of the ministers sent by Jean Calvin to participate in the establishment of Villegaignon's ill-fated colony in Brazil, wrote his own account of the enterprise in 1578. Here Léry accused the Catholic Thevet of being little more than an "impudent liar" in blaming Protestants for the colony's failure and asserted that his works were "second-hand rags

7. North America is described in the second volume, fols. 984 to 1020. An English translation is given in Schlesinger and Stabler, *André Thevet's North America*, 27–69, 134–58, 172–215.

8. Hoffman, in *Cabot to Cartier: Sources for a Historical Ethnography of Northeastern North America, 1497–1550* (Toronto, 1961), 178–79 and table 7, examined these "conversations" and concluded that all but two of Thevet's phrases derive from the vocabularies in Jacques Cartier's *Brief Récit*.

and tatters."[9] Just as religious differences motivated Léry's hostility to Thevet, so, too, can an ulterior motive be found in François de Belleforest's criticisms. These authors had published cosmographies within months of each other in 1575, and neither missed an opportunity to attack the integrity and credibility of a rival. Belleforest, for example, accused Thevet of stealing material from his work, while Thevet correctly pointed out that Belleforest, who had never traveled to the New World, of necessity had to rely on others for his information.[10] In fact, both Thevet and Belleforest encountered the censure of Richard Hakluyt, the celebrated English compiler of travel accounts, who offered the judgment that both wrote "wearie volumes bearing the titles of universall Cosmographie which some men that I could name have published as their owne, beyng in deed most untruly and unprofitablie ramassed and hurled together."[11] Henri Lancelot de Voisin, sieur de la Popelinière, echoed this judgment when he asserted that both Thevet and Belleforest wrote not for the public interest but their own profit, "which they obtained by the miserable work of their unbridled pens."[12]

In evaluating Thevet's status as an expert on the New World, succeeding generations of scholars contented themselves with repeating the judgments of Léry, Belleforest, Hakluyt, and La Popelinière. Indeed, Jacques-Auguste de Thou, a contemporary famed for his impartial approach to the events of his own time, offered an even more critical description of Thevet in his *Histoire universelle*:

> [He] applied himself to writing books, which he sold to miserable publishers: after having compiled extracts of different authors, he added to them everything he could find in road guides and other such books, which are in popular hands. In fact, more ignorant than you could possibly conceive and having no acquaintanceship with

9.    "*vieux haillons et fripperies*"; see Léry's preface to *Histoire d'un voyage* (1578 ed.).

10.   For examples see Belleforest's edited and enlarged French version of Sebastian Münster's *Cosmographia universalis*, 2 vols. (Paris, 1575), 2:cols. 2039–40; and Thevet's complaints about Belleforest in his letter to Abraham Ortelius in J. H. Hessels, *Ecclesiae londino-batavae archivum*, vol. 1, *Abrahami Ortelli epistulae* (Cambridge, U.K., 1887), 329–30.

11.   Preface "To the Reader," *Principal Navigations* (1589) in *The Original Writings and Correspondence of the Two Richard Hakluyts*, introduction and notes by E. G. R. Taylor, 2 vols. (London, 1935), 2:402.

12.   Henri Lancelot de Voisin, *L'histoire des histoires* (Paris, 1599), 455–58.

literature, nor antiquity, nor chronology, he put in his books the uncertain for the certain, the false for the true, with an astonishing assurance. I remember that some of my friends, clever people with a keen wit, having gone one day to see him to amuse themselves, made him believe in my presence ridiculous and absurd things, which children even would have trouble swallowing; which made me laugh a lot. I can therefore not keep from pitying some people who, although well-versed in the sciences, not only do not perceive his stupidities of a charlatan, but cite him every day with honor in their writings. I have often been astonished that a man so easily fooled, has himself fooled persons of such great reputation. I therefore warn them now to no longer in the future dishonor their works by citing an author so ignorant and contemptible.[13]

Brief critical accounts in the eighteenth century, for example those of Jacob le Duchat and J.-P. Nicéron, repeated the typical accusations of Thevet's ignorance and mendacity.[14] By the nineteenth century George Dexter, in the fourth volume of Justin Winsor's *Narrative and Critical History of America*, claimed that Thevet's "reputation for truth-telling is so poor that many historians are inclined to reject altogether his recital of the voyage along our coast," while the *Nouvelle biographie générale*, a standard reference, concluded in 1866 that Thevet's works had fallen into a "well-deserved oblivion."[15]

That judgment lasted for only little more than a decade, however; revisionist interpretations of Thevet's worth soon began to appear. In 1878 Paul Gaffarel began the rehabilitation of Thevet's reputation with a new, annotated edition of *Singularitez* and continued it with a biographical article ten years later.[16] These two contributions, together with another short biography by Marcellino Da Civezza

---

13.  Jacques-Auguste de Thou, *Histoire universelle*, 16 vols. (London, 1734), 2:651–52.

14.  Jacob le Duchat, *Satyre Menippée de la vertu du catholicon d'Espagne*, ed. P. Marchand, 3 vols. (Regensberg, 1711), 2:285; and *Les bibliothèques Françoises de la Croix du Maine et Du Verdier*, new ed., 6 vols. (Paris, 1771–72, repr. Graz, Austria, 1969), 1:21–22; J.-P. Nicéron, *Mémoires pour servir à l'histoire des hommes illustres dans la republique des lettres*, 43 vols. (Paris, 1729-45), 23 (1733):74–83.

15.  Dexter, "Cortereal, Verrazano, Gomez, Thevet," 4:1–32 (quotation 12); Jean C. F. Hoefer, ed., *Nouvelle biographie générale* 45 (1866):col. 128.

16.  Gaffarel's 1878 edition of *Singularitez* included a "Notice biographique" of Thevet (v–xxxiii) that he revised and published in *Bulletin de Géographie Historique et Descriptive* (1888):166–201.

(who used the unpublished notes of Ferdinand Denis),[17] summarized and presented in scholarly form what was known about Thevet until 1905. At that time Edouard de Jonghe first revealed Thevet's materials on Aztec civilization, still considered among the best written outside Spain and the Indies, in his "Histoyre du Mechique, manuscrit français inédit du XVIe siécle" and "Thevet, Mexicaniste."[18] Two years later Daniel Touzard defended Thevet's claim to have introduced tobacco into France, and in 1911 Gilbert Chinard noted the considerable influence Thevet exerted on French conceptions of the Native American.[19]

Estevão Pinto and Jean Adhémar continued to rehabilitate Thevet in the 1940s. In 1943 Pinto published "O Franciscano André Thevet," the first scholarly article on Thevet in Portuguese, followed in 1944 by his translation of *Singularitez* into the same language. Inspired by Pinto, Manoel da Silveira Cardozo offered the first important account of Thevet's career in English.[20] A few years later Adhémar, who had already published "André Thevet collectioneur de portraits,"[21] wrote a full-length biography of Thevet, *Frère André Thevet, grand voyageur et cosmographe des rois de France au xvie siècle* (Paris, 1947). Unfortunately, Adhémar treated his subject rather uncritically and failed to cite his sources. Six years later, Suzanne Lussagnet presented *Le Brésil et les Brésiliens par André Thevet*,[22] an important study for promoting research on Thevet. It contains the Brazilian sections of *Cosmographie universelle* and two previously unpublished manuscripts, "Histoire de deux voyages" and "Grand Insulaire,"[23]

17.   Da Civezza, "André Thevet," 590–94.

18.   In *Journal de la Société des Américanistes de Paris*, n.s. 2 (1905):1–41 and *International Congress of Americanists* (1906):223–40 respectively.

19.   Touzard, "André Thevet d'Angoulesme," 1–47; Chinard, *L'exotisme Américain*, chap. 4.

20.   Pinto's article appeared in *Cultura Politica* 3 (1943):118–36; Estevão Pinto, ed., *Singularidades da França Antarctica a que outros chamam de America* (São Paulo, 1944); Silveira Cardozo, "Some Remarks Concerning André Thevet," 15–36.

21.   In *Revue Archéologique* (1942–43):41–54.

22.   Lussagnet, *Les Français en Amérique*.

23.   "Histoire d'André Thevet angoumoisin, cosmographe du roy, de deux voyages par luy faits aux Indes australes et occidentales. . . . " (1588, BN MS fr. 15454); "Le grand insulaire et pilotage d'André Thevet angoumoisin, cosmographe du roy. . . . " (1586?, 2 vols., BN MS fr. 15452 and 15453).

and continues to be a standard reference.

While Lussagnet reaffirmed the importance of Thevet's descriptions of Brazil and the Tupinamba, in the 1930s William F. Ganong began to establish Thevet's reputation as an authentic source for sixteenth-century Canada. Ganong's work, however, did not become readily available until it was collected and published as *Crucial Maps in the Early Cartography and Place-Nomenclature of the Atlantic Coast of Canada*, edited by Theodore E. Layng, in 1964. Ganong emphasized that Thevet's text was taken ultimately from oral sources and consequently contained important, original, and accurate information. The far-reaching influence of Ganong's reinterpretation can be clearly seen in the work of Bernard G. Hoffman, who concluded that "Thevet's description of Canada contains original information obtained verbally from Cartier himself, which could not have been invented by any stretch of the imagination and which is subject to check."[24]

Most recently, scholars have focused on specific aspects of Thevet's work and have also edited and translated most of his geographical texts. Important studies include those by Marcel Destombes, Rüdiger Joppien, P. E. H. Hair, Janet Whatley, and, of course, Lestringant.[25] In addition to writing persuasive and original studies on Thevet's career from various perspectives, Lestringant published new editions of *Singularitez* (1983) and *Cosmographie de Levant* (1985). Jean Baudry also published a facsimile edition of *Singularitez* (1982) with a useful introduction. Finally, Eugenio Amado translated *Singularitez* into Portuguese in 1978, and Roger Schlesinger and Arthur P. Stabler produced an annotated, English translation of several of Thevet's accounts of North America, including a portion of the previously unpublished "Grand Insulaire," in 1986.[26]

24.  Hoffman, *Cabot to Cartier*, 171–72.

25.  Destombes, "André Thevet (1504–1592)," 123–31; Joppien, "Etude de quelques portraits," 125–36; Hair, "A Note on Thevet's Unpublished Maps," 105–16; Whatley, "Savage Hierarchies." Some of Lestringant's more important works are listed in the Bibliography of this volume. Unfortunately, we have not been able to consult *André Thevet, cosmographe des derniers Valois* (Geneva, 1991), which appeared after this book went to press.

26.  Jean Baudry, *Les singularités de la France Antarctique* (Paris, 1982); Eugenio Amado, *As singularidades da França Antarctica* (São Paulo, 1978); Schlesinger and Stabler, *André Thevet's North America*.

The result of this scholarship has been the emergence of a more intelligent and balanced assessment of Thevet's work. Marcel Trudel, for example, summarized the prevailing attitude when he described Thevet as "a bogus scholar and a naïve compiler of facts," but he also admitted that information supplied by Thevet, often resting on no known written source, has been proved accurate by present-day scholars.[27] More recently, Olive P. Dickason ranked Thevet with Léry and Hans Staden as the period's leading sources of New World ethnographic data and declared that he "casts his net wider than the other two, who confined their attentions to Brazilians. Thevet not only added flesh to the bare bones of Cartier's published observations, but also pondered entrepreneurial prospects of New France that Cartier must have considered but did not record."[28]

### Les vrais pourtraits et vies des hommes illustres

The debate over Thevet's scholarship has centered on his geographical works. Ironically, he regarded *Vrais pourtraits* as the culmination of his career and went into debt to finance its printing.[29] The book is a collection of 232 biographical sketches, each illustrated with an engraved portrait of its subject.[30] Thevet devoted the first volume, containing eighty-three entries, to "personnages signalez pour la rarité de leur sçavoir." In the second, containing 149 entries,[31] he described the lives of warriors, navigators and sea captains, lawyers,

27. Marcel Trudel, "André Thevet," in *Dictionary of Canadian Biography*, ed. G. W. Brown and Marcel Trudel (Toronto, 1966), 1:680.

28. Olive P. Dickason, *The Myth of the Savage and the Beginnings of French Colonialism in the Americas* (Edmonton, 1984), 178.

29. *Les vrais pourtaits et vies des hommes illustres*; a Facsimile Re-edition with introduction by Rouben C. Cholakian (Delmar, N.Y., 1973), viii. Publication was also supported by the Florentine Jean-Baptiste Bencivenni, Catherine de Medici's librarian (Balmas, *Documenti inediti*, 56).

30. Ten chapters lack portraits (1:chaps. 45, 60, 76, 78; 2:chaps. 46, 59, 88, 119, 121, 127). Adhémar listed 221 portraits, omitting Aristotle's and giving provenance when he knew it, in *Inventaire du fonds*, 114–19.

31. The last chapter of the second volume is numbered 150, but chapters 9, 10, and 51 are missing while there are two chapters each numbered 28 and 29, for a net loss of one chapter. The table of contents of the second volume, where the errors occur, has 150 entries only because Horace is listed twice, under *H* and *Q* (Q. Horace Flace [*sic*]).

orators, doctors, and a few artisans. Like other Renaissance biographers, Thevet included figures from antiquity and the Middle Ages in his work, but *Vrais pourtraits* is distinguished by its high percentage of biographies of contemporaries, particularly individuals from Asia, Africa, and the Americas. The selection of so many non-Europeans reflected his own interests in geography and ethnography, and it fed the reading public's growing appetite for information about strange people living in far-off lands.[32]

Thevet's use of copperplate engravings also distinguishes *Vrais pourtraits* from many other Renaissance collections of biographies. In fact, Jean Adhémar, Thevet's biographer, went so far as to assert that "this will be less a biographical than an iconographical dictionary, a succession of portraits of famous men, each accompanied by a short note on the life and works of the person represented. The note will be brief, it is but an accessory, the important thing is the portrait."[33]

Obviously, *Vrais pourtraits* is the logical culmination of Thevet's life-long interest in book illustration. *Singularitez*, for example, his first work on America, has been described as one of the most beautiful French books of the sixteenth century: "Whether we speak of their documentary interest or their artistic merit, of their greatness or of the life which we see in them, Thevet's illustrations surpass all other sixteenth-century works of art on America. The care lavished on the work[s] bears ample witness to the importance Thevet attached to their publication."[34]

After using woodcut illustrations so effectively in *Singularitez*, Thevet continued his practice by incorporating them, some in modified form, in *Cosmographie universelle*. He also included new woodcuts in the latter. Of particular interest here are the portraits of Quoniambec (fig. 1) and "Un Roy des Cannibales" (fig. 2), each of which reappear in *Vrais pourtraits* much improved because of the new technology of book illustration.

Although several authors already had made good use of copperplate engraving by the middle of the sixteenth century, Thevet's use

32. Chinard, *L'exotisme Américain*; Atkinson, *Les nouveaux horizons*.

33. Adhémar, "Thevet collectionneur," 46.

34. Joppien, "Etude de quelques portraits," 126.

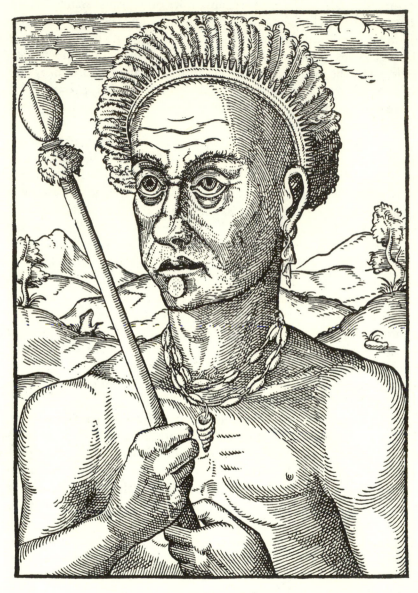

Figure 1. Quoniambec

Figure 2. "Roy du Promontoire des Cannibales"

of it helped popularize the new method.[35] In typical immodest fashion he declared in the Preface to *Vrais pourtraits*: "I was obliged to seek out the engravers I had heard were expert, well trained and skilled in drawing from life and representing naturally the look of the people whom I proposed. Toward this end, I had to bring the best engravers I could find from Flanders, and I was so successful that I may boast of being the first to make copperplate engraving as stylish in Paris as it already was at Lyon, Antwerp, and elsewhere."[36] Nevertheless, even if Thevet exaggerated his own importance, he certainly championed the use of copperplate engraving, and *Vrais pourtraits* contributed significantly to its popularity.[37]

Thevet used a variety of sources to ensure that his portraits were accurate, including royal, aristocratic, and ecclesiastical collections. He described this diligent search for authentic materials in the Preface of *Vrais pourtraits*: "In order to make the reader feel the truth of what I say, everybody knows how hard I have worked to gather and order the portraits which I reproduce here, and whether the expense would not have discouraged anybody else who had tried to bring such a daring enterprise to fruition. For my own part, I can assure the reader of having visited most libraries and shops, French as well as foreign, in order to recover, to the extent possible, all the rare objects [*rarités & singularités*] which I knew to be necessary to accomplish my aim." Further evidence of Thevet's desire for authenticity is his letter of 1584 to Monsieur Ronat, "Avocat au Parlement." Explaining that he had discarded the engraving of La Trémouille after it was already done, he noted that he decided to use a second portrait provided by the queen mother, even though doing so doubled his expenses for that illustration.[38]

35. A detailed account of the history of book illustration in France is in Brun, *Le livre Français illustré*, esp. 95–102.

36. Brun cites this passage as "being of capital importance for the history of engraving in France" (100–101).

37. Joppien, "Etude de quelques portraits," 132. Laterally reversed derivatives of Thevet's portraits of Columbus, Vespucci, Magellan, and Cortés appeared in Isaac Bullart's *Academie des sciences et des arts, contenant les vies, & les eloges historiques des hommes illustres*, 2 vols. (Amsterdam and Brussels, 1682), 2:265, 273, 275, 277.

38. "Lettre d'André Thevet à Ronet," in *Mélanges de littérature et d'histoire* (Paris, 1877), item 6.

Jean Adhémar and Jean Baudry, comparing the engravings in *Vrais pourtraits* to other known likenesses, concluded that Thevet's efforts to provide authentic portraits proved generally successful.[39] Moreover, some of them preserved iconographic data that otherwise would have perished, in the same way that his prose has preserved some ethnographic descriptions. To cite one example, he copied the portrait of Jean d'Orléans, count of Angoulême, from a stained glass window in the Celestine Church in Paris, which no longer exists.[40]

Thevet consulted a vast array of source materials to glean information about the great variety of peoples, places, and times covered in *Vrais pourtraits*. We can infer some of his sources, although he almost never acknowledged them himself. For instance, he used Amyot's translation of Plutarch's *Lives* (Paris, 1559) for his figures from the ancient world and Trithemius's *De scriptoribus ecclesiasticis* (Paris, 1512) for his medieval ecclesiastics.[41] He also relied on Paolo Giovio's *Elogia veris clarorum virorum* (Venice, 1546), which was translated into Italian by Lodovico Domenichi in 1554 and into French by Blaise d'Everon in 1559.[42] Thevet also used his own collection of materials, which he had compiled during his travels and which he described in *Cosmographie universelle*.[43] The importance of these items cannot be exaggerated; he used his position as royal cosmographer to collect rare documents and artifacts. Of special significance is the *Codex Mendoza*, an illustrated history of the Aztecs detailing political and social events and customs from the establishment of Tenochtitlan in 1324 until the Spanish conquest in 1519.[44] This invaluable account of native life apparently came into Thevet's possession when the French intercepted the ship carrying the *Codex* to Spain. Richard Hakluyt,

---

39. Adhémar, "Thevet collectioneur," 53; *Singularitez*, ed. Baudry, 52–54.

40. Cholakian, "Introduction," *Vrais pourtraits*, xi; also see f.300r.

41. Adhémar (*Frère André Thevet*, 60) also mentions unspecified works by Gesner and Leland as sources.

42. Giovio, *Gli elogi vite brevemente* includes the epitaphs for Columbus and Cortés that Thevet used, but d'Everon's *Les éloges et vies briefvement descrites . . . .* (Paris, 1559) does not. We have used the Venice, 1557 edition of Domenichi's Italian translation.

43. 2:f.471r.

44. The best modern edition of the *Codex* is James Cooper Clark, *The Mexican Manuscript Known as the Collection of Mendoza and Preserved in the Bodleian Library Oxford*, 3 vols. (London, 1938).

when in Paris in 1587, bought it from Thevet for twenty French crowns, and Samuel Purchas later published it as the "choisest of my jewels."[45]

A second French edition of *Vrais pourtraits* appeared in Paris in 1670–71, under the title *Histoire des plus illustres et sçavans hommes*, and was reissued in 1695.[46] The addition of more contemporary figures enlarged this work and necessitated its division into eight smaller volumes, "for greater ease, because such curious works, of which the subject matter is so easily divided, are as suited to the countryside or solitary walks as they are to the study, and also because the reader is less tired if he can hold them in his hand than if he has to lower his gaze to a desk."[47] In 1973, Scholars' Facsimiles and Reprints issued a reproduction of the 1584 *Vrais pourtraits* with a useful introduction in English by Rouben C. Cholakian, but with no annotations to the text.

Twenty-seven of Thevet's biographical sketches have been translated into English. In 1657, George Gerbier, "alias D'Ovvilly," translated twenty chapters to add to North's Plutarch under the title *Prosopographia: or, some select pourtraitures and lives of ancient and modern illustrious personages* and added five others when the work reappeared in 1676.[48] Since that time, only two other biographies by Thevet have been translated into English, those of Paraousti Satouriona, king of Florida, and Johannes Guttenberg. Neither are annotated.[49]

45. *Hakluytus Posthumus, or Purchas his pilgrimes*, 15:412–504. For an account of Hakluyt's purchase of the *Codex* from Thevet, see D. B. Quinn, *The Hakluyt Handbook*, 2 vols. (London, 1974), 1:294–95.

46. *Histoire des plus illustres et sçavans hommes de leurs siecles. Tant de l'Europe que de l'Asie, Afrique & Amerique. Avec leurs portraits en tailles-douçes, tirez sur les veritables originaux*, 8 vols. (Paris, 1670–71).

47. 2:"Le Libraire au Lecteur."

48. *Prosopographia*. . . . was added to *The lives of the noble Grecians and Romans, compared together, by that grave learned philosopher and historiographer Plutarch of Chaerona. Translated out of Greek into French, by James Amiot . . . and out of French into English, by Sir Thomas North, knight*. The 1657 edition contained translations of Thevet's chapters on Constantine the Great, Archimedes, Diogenes, Constantine Paleologus, Justinian, Aristotle, Homer, Sapho, Saladin, Edward (Prince of Wales), Charlemagne, Tamberlain, Priscian, Artemesia, Terrence, Hismael Sophi, Georges Castriot, Tamombeus, Atabalipa, and Guttenberg. The 1676 edition added Cortés, Basil (Duke of Moscovy), Sebastian I (of Portugal), Quoniambec, and Columbus.

49. Bennett, *Laudonnière and Fort Caroline*, esp. 171–76; and *Jean Guttemberg, Inventor of*

This volume presents annotated English translations of the twelve biographies in *Vrais pourtraits* that are devoted to European explorers and American natives. The descriptions of early European explorers are particularly interesting because they reveal the extent of Thevet's knowledge, based on his wide reading in the travel literature of the time and on his own experiences in the New World, of the exploits of Pizarro, Cortés, Albuquerque, Columbus, Vespucci, and Magellan. The other six chapters contain Thevet's pioneering biographies of Native Americans: Atabalipa (Atahuallpa), Montezuma, Nacol-absou "King of the Promontory of Cannibals," Paracoussi "King of Plata," Quoniambec (Konyan Bebe), and Paarousti Satouriona (Satouriwa). Much of the information in the chapters on Native Americans derives from his own experiences in America and from stories he had heard from others. For this reason, they are certainly the most original and probably the most interesting and important of the *Vrais pourtraits*.[50]

Taken together, these twelve chapters provide a unique example of the information disseminated about the Age of Exploration and the New World in late sixteenth-century Europe, especially in France. Above all, they bear witness to the ways these data, often quite surprising, could be coded so as to be comprehensible to contemporary readers. Therefore, their significance does not depend solely upon their truthfulness. As Tzvetan Todorov put it, "The reception of utterances is more revelatory of the history of ideologies than is their production. When an author makes a mistake—or lies—the text is no less important than when it tells the truth; the important thing is that the text be understandable to contemporaries [*recevable par les contemporains*], or that it has been believed to be so by its producer. From this point of view, the notion of 'false' is irrelevant [*non pertinent*]."[51]

*Printing*, tr. D. C. McMurtrie (New York, 1926).

50. In 1958, Borba de Moraes noted that *Vrais pourtraits* "had not been a much searched for book until of late when its American contents became better known, and its price has increased accordingly." *Bibliographia Brasiliana*, 2:307.

51. Tzvetan Todorov, *La conquête de l'Amérique: La question de l'autre* (Paris, 1982), 60.

A NOTE ON THE TRANSLATION AND ANNOTATIONS

We have attempted to translate Thevet's sixteenth-century French into modern English without destroying or improving the character of the original prose. We have used Thevet's marginal rubrics as headings in place of modern paragraphs, sometimes inserting them into the middle of sentences when his placement seemed to call for it. Thevet's capitalization, use of italics, and accent marks have been retained, although we have occasionally added a word or two for clarity and have changed the spelling of a few proper nouns (e.g., Pizarro and Cortés). We have limited our annotations to items of special interest, and footnotes or editorial explications (e.g., Paly [Palos]) usually appear only at the first mention of an item. Folio numbers appearing throughout the text in brackets refer to the original 1584 edition of *Vrais pourtraits*. Short citations occur in the footnotes when the source appears in the Bibliography.

# I

## European Explorers

## FRANCOIS PISARRE.

### Chapitre 52.

 A conqueſte du nouueau monde eſt cele-
bréepar pluſieurs, qui ſe mirent ſeulement
aux threſors, delices & precieux ioyaux, qui
ont eſté apportés de là. De ma part ie ſigne-
ray touſiours auec les autres, que cela rend
telles conqueſtes grandement recomman-
dables, mais auſſi i'eſtime, que, ſans faire tort
à ces tant renommés cõquereurs, on ne doit
attacher l'excellence de telles conqueſtes ſeulement à l'or, pierreries
& richeſſes, qui en ont eſté tirées, mais qu'il faut y conioindre enſem-

*Conqueſta du nouueau monde en quoy ſont à priſer.*

RRr iiij

# Francisco Pizarro

Many have celebrated the conquest of the new world solely for the treasures and precious jewels which have been brought from there. For my part, I shall always side with the others, who hold that such riches render the conquests noteworthy but, without detracting from the feats of such famous conquerors, surely all the merit of their conquests does not reside in the gold, jewels, and riches brought back from them, but also resides necessarily [374v] in the prowess and feats of the officers who risked their lives to discover and conquer countries unknown to our fathers.

### In what ways the conquerors are worthy of praise

To tell the truth, I find the aforementioned relationship quite fitting, in as much as the great abundance of gold and wealth which existed naturally in this country was only prized by Europeans when its musky odor reached our nostrils, in the same way that the valor of the Conquerors would have been shrouded in obscurity, had it not been awakened by their feats during the conquests, embalming Europe and all the rest of the world with the exhalation of heroism from so many, and such successful, conquests. I do not mean to say, however, that the Europeans gained their skills from these Americans, since I hold, on the contrary, that the latter served merely as a paper, bronze, or marble upon which to inscribe the immortal memory of their deeds.

### The father of Francisco Pizarro

Lest I stray from the subject of the present discourse, the heroism of Pizarro, I wonder whether you think it would have been as well known had it been limited to Spain for its display—where I have no doubt that he would have offered excellent proof of his nobility, since he was the son of the famous Gonzales Pizarro, Governor of the Kingdom of Navarre, even though some have let it be rumored that Francisco was a bastard son of whom Gonzales took so little account that he set Francisco to pig farming. According to Girolamo Benzoni (who is doing no more than repeating what some as ill-informed as he is told him)[1] some of his pigs disappeared one day, with the result that Francisco no longer dared return home, and fled to Seville. From there, he went to the Indies with Captain Alfonso de Hoieda [Ojeda], who had been named Governor of the Province of Urana [Uraba]. The story is not true, even if it is funny, and I am surprised that Prince Chauveton let himself be duped by it.[2] He might well have guessed that, in order to make the tale plausible, he would have had to distance Pizarro from his vocation as swineherd.

### Agreement between three Spaniards for the trip to the Indies

Let us leave these detractors and return to our Pizarro, whose undertaking is quite otherwise reported by the same author, who remarks that Pizarro made an agreement and contract with two other Spaniards living in the city of Panama, to wit Diego d'Almagro and a priest named Fernand de Luques. They outfitted two ships, on which Pizarro and D'Almagro embarked with two hundred twenty soldiers in the year 1526.

1.   Thevet here is most likely referring to Benzoni's principal source, Francicso López de Gómara, who wrote *Historia general de las Indias*.... (pt. 1 of *La Istoria de las Indias y conquista de Mexico* [Zaragoza, 1552]). The notes to the Spanish translation of Benzoni's work by Vannini de Gerulewicz provide a detailed comparison of the two works.

2.   Urbain Chauveton, a Huguenot scholar, translated Benzoni's work into Latin (1578) and French (1579).

## Francisco Pizarro and d'Almagro
### defeated by the Indians

The priest stayed home, and the others would have been better off to
do likewise; they would not have been beaten black and blue as they
were by the Indians, who charged them [375r] again and again, for all
the reinforcements which were sent from time to time from Panama.
They were so heartily received that there were precious few in the
company who were eager to test their welcome any further. In fact,
after d'Almagro's departure to bring reinforcements back, Pizarro
was forced, by order of Pedro de los Rios, governor of Panama, to
allow those who wished to do so to return to Spain. He did so, and
found himself alone with fourteen men on the Isle du Coq [Isla del
Gallo].

## The discovery of Chira

With this tiny handful of men, Pizarro tempted fate, made a five
hundred mile trip and came out in a part of Peru called Chira. None
of them dared look around save a certain Candiot [Pietro de Candia],
who found such a great treasure that Pizarro and his men took heart.

## Pizarro granted the conquest
### and government of Peru

It was for this reason that Pizarro returned to Spain, to ask for
the conquest and government of Peru, by which he promised sub-
stantially to augment the treasury of the Crown of Castille. He
obtained all he asked.[3] He made himself ready and left there with
four brothers, to wit Ferdinand, Gonzales, and Juan Pizarro and
Martin d'Alcantara.

---

3. Thevet is less critical of Pizarro's conduct than Benzoni: "On arriving in Spain he
presented himself to the Council of the Indies, and after describing to them the countries
that *he* had found, and the expense which *he* had incurred, as well as the hardships that *he*
had undergone, and promising very great treasures to the crown of Castile, he asked for
the government and the conquest of *Tumbes* for himself only, without making the slightest
mention of his companions." See Benzoni's *Historia del Mondo Nuovo*; we have used the
English translation *History of the New World*, ed. and trans. Smyth, 174.

### Beginning of conflict between
### Francisco Pizarro and Almagro

His companions had no sooner discovered the agreement than they began to argue, especially d'Almagro, who was nonetheless finally appeased by Doctor [Antonio de la] Gama, who made up for Pizarro's perfidy and overweening errors the best he could.

### Conquest of the Isle of Puna and of Tumbez

The latter, supported by the troops and treasure of Don Diego, embarked with one hundred fifty soldiers and many horse, and landed at Colonchy, a port of the province of Guancanilichi [Huancavelica]. From there he passed to the Isle of Puna, where he attacked the hapless Indians with terrible fury, for all the courtesy they showed him. The inhabitants of Tumbez fared no better; he took and sacked the city, especially the beautiful Temple to the Sun which was there.

### Atabalipa [Atahuallpa] tries to deny
### Pizarro entry to his country

Atabalipa, hearing of the entry of these bearded ones into his country, began to react to it: he gave them an ultimatum to depart, or he would attack them. They advanced as far as they could, for all the remonstrations of the unhappy king of Peru, and at last arrived before Cassiamalgue [Caxamalca], where Atabalipa arrived with great pomp. As he arrived at the palace, to give public audience to his people, a friar [Vicente de Valverde] from Pizarro's party presented himself in behalf of Pizarro, to remind the king of the duty he owed the Pope and many other great leaders with which I shall not burden this tale. The king replied so fiercely that the Spaniards immediately let fly with their artillery, which buzzed so that the poor Indians, who were more than twenty-five thousand strong, stunned by the thunder of the guns and the furious neighing of the horses, [375v] allowed themselves to be slaughtered, making only token resistance.

## CAPTURE AND DEATH OF ATABALIPA

Francisco Pizarro stormed through the crowd straight to Attabalipa, who was surrounded by a great number of Indians. The fire on this crowd was so heavy that Atabalipa's bearers were already beginning to waiver. Pizarro advanced, grabbed the unhappy king by his shirt tails, and dragged him [Atahuallpa] with him. He reached an agreement on his ransom, which was truly paid in full. Nonetheless, against his solemn word (and he has been quite rightfully criticized by many who find it hard to swallow an officer and gentleman's taking so little account of his sworn word of honor), Pizarro put Atabalipa to death, the better to invade his lands, and because a dead dog neither barks nor bites. After his death, several pretenders raised their heads: among others Quisquis, the commander in chief of the dead king's armies, but none had the resources to resist Pizarro.

## DEATH OF DON DIEGO ALMAGRO

The latter puffed himself up over his victories, such as they were, but he quickly found an obstacle to occupy all his energy: his enmity of long standing with Don Diego Almagro. The latter, having obtained the post of Governor [*Mareschal*] of Peru from the emperor Charles V, thought to use his title to constrain Pizarro.[4] Almagro found himself so frustrated instead, though, that he found himself forced to leave the country and, after having wandered around Chile in search of the treasure rumored to be hidden there, found himself obliged to leave his own life as security. In the meantime, Francisco's brother Ferdinand had brought tidings of the Emperor's award of the title of Marquis to him [Francisco]. Don Diego's life was more fully avenged than Atabalipa's though, for Juan de Rada [Herrada] joined with eleven soldiers fully committed to paying him back for the indignities he visited upon Almagro's supporters, after Ferdinand caused Don Diego to be strangled and decapitated in prison—the same Diego who had, as they say, rescued him from the gallows.

4. Benzoni's account again is less sympathetic to Pizarro: "[Almagro] began to share out the Indians in his own way. But Pizarro hearing of it, immediately sent his brother John, with some other Spaniards, ordering them to oppose Almagro's making any alteration whatever in the country without his permission." Ibid., 185–86.

They crossed the square crying *Long live the king—and death to the tyrant!*[5] They broke into the Marquis Pizarro's house, where they made a fearful slaughter of all who tried to stop them from executing their plan.

## DEATH OF FRANCISCO PIZARRO

Captain Francisco de Chiaves, who was guarding the door, Doctor Valasquez, Martin d'Alcantara (Pizarro's elder brother), and finally our own Francisco Pizarro all stayed there. Francisco fought back for a long time, but was finally overwhelmed, particularly by one assailant who had no desire whatever for him to survive. He slashed Francisco in the throat, of which he dropped dead.[6] After his death, the Almagristes left and elected Diego's son to the governorship of Peru, before the Emperor could take other steps. They had [376r] so embittered the Peruvians as well as the Spaniards against Pizarro and his supporters that it was very unsafe for them to be in the country.

## GONZALES PIZARRO GOVERNOR AND PROTECTOR OF PERU

For this reason Gonzales Pizarro withdrew quietly to his mines in the province of Ciarches [Las Charcas], where he was minding his own business. He was recalled, however, by Conquistadores in the capital and elsewhere who were disturbed by the conduct of Blasco Nunez, who had been sent to Peru by the Emperor in the year 1540. The Conquistadores unanimously begged Lord Gonzales to declare himself governor general and protector of Peru, which he could not refuse them. Many rebelled against the violence of the Viceroy, and gave him a lot to think about, for he was unable to gain the upper hand over Pizarro by either the most harsh or the most conciliatory gestures.

---

5.   Thevet's quotation follows Benzoni, ibid., 198.

6.   According to Prescott, Pizarro cried "Jesus" as he fell, then drew a cross on the ground in his own blood and kissed it before he died. See *The History of the Conquest of Peru*, 2:172.

## DEATH OF BLASCO NUNEZ, VICEROY OF PERU

Executions caught the unwary on both sides, to the point that the Viceroy Blasco lost his own life a league outside the city of Quito, where he was killed by a slave of Barrister Carvaial [Carvajal] to avenge the death of his brother whom Blasco had stabbed in anger in Lima. The Emperor sent Pedro de la Gasca with two lieutenants, Cienca [Andrés de Cianca] and Rienterio [Rentería], to still these quarrels in 1546.

## DEATH OF GONZALES PIZARRO

These two used the fox-tail with which they covered themselves so skillfully that they made it seem like a lion-skin; Pizarro was defeated with his men and taken by a gentleman named Villa-vicentio [Villa Vicenza], the sergeant major of the Emperor's camp, then passed to president Gasca, who, after having reminded him of how far he had exceeded his authority in taking up arms against his majesty, handed him over to Barrister Cianca to finish his prosecution. The latter found him guilty of treason both against the state and against the person of the king. The next day, in execution of the sentence against him, he was mounted on a mule saddled and bridled, with his hands tied, and was covered with a cape. He was decapitated in Cusco, and his head was carried and placed in the city of the kings, on a marble pillar surrounded by an iron fence, with this inscription: *This is the head of the traitor Gonzales Pizarro.*[7] His body was buried in Cusco, and this execution was carried out on the ninth of April in 1548.

## DEFENSE OF THE AUTHOR AGAINST SOME CRITICS

This does not invalidate what I said in the fourteenth [sixteenth] chapter of the twenty- second book of my Cosmographie, that Pizarro, fleeing from the fury of the Lord of Mendozza [Mendoza] and other Spaniards, lost his ships, since Don Anthony de Mendozza had not been sent to Mexico as Viceroy until the time of Ferdinand Cortés,

7. The account here of Gonzales Pizarro's death appears in Benzoni's narrative, but the inscription is found only in Gómara, *Historia general de las Indias*, 2:179.

and was later sent to govern Peru. This does not rule out his having hunted down Gonzales Pizarro; [376v] since, if my lord Mendozza was Viceroy of Mexico in the year 1539 and thereafter, is it outside the bounds of possibility that he ran into Pizarro, who was not so preoccupied with his mines that he was not always looking for new fish to fry? If the author who reports a massacre of some Frenchmen exploring Florida had cleaned out his ears, he would not have made the mistaken allusion by which he presumes to impute a false report to me.[8] The problem may be that he supposes that I meant to say that my lord Mendozza brought Gonzales Pizarro to the bar, which would be an even bigger mistake on his part, since any sane man will not find in the passage that he took from my Cosmographie that Gonzales was sentenced by my lord Mendozza. In fact, the words *which was executed in time* do give an impression which I did not intend that the capture of Gonzales coincided with Mendozza's charge against him. The evidence is nonetheless clear that the passage truly means no more than that Gonzales was executed during the administration of this President [Judge] Gasca.

### Error of those who would place twelve hundred leagues between Peru and Mexico

The impudence of this raver is even more excessive when he, having spent most of his life in his cups (as they say), undertakes to utter pronouncements on distances between places which he has not only never been, but which he has perhaps not even examined on the marine maps which he praises so highly. Had he examined these maps, they would have taught him what I have observed carefully, the size of Mexico as well as Peru. If he were able to see at all, he would discover how mistaken he was to put more than twelve

---

8. Thevet is referring to Chauveton, who added to his translations of Benzoni, *Brief discours et histoire d'un voyage de quelques François en la Floride: et du massacre autant iniustement que barbarement executé sur eux, par les Hespagnols, l'an mil cenq cens soixante cinq.* In *Histoire nouvelle du nouveau monde* (Geneva, 1579). Chauveton concluded his critique of Thevet's *Cosmographie universelle* (2:f.994r) by observing, "We thus see Thevet's arrogant ignorance: he would have done better to learn from others, and to confess openly from whom he got what he says, instead of lying like a defrocked priest, and trying to make everyone believe that he has been everywhere and that he has not reaped the harvest others sowed" (38).

hundred leagues between them. I shall not belabor him with the fact that many have so amply inflated the borders of Peru that it became thirteen hundred leagues long: he is unaware that the correct description of Peru shows that it could not be more than seven hundred leagues long, from North to South, and one hundred wide, from East to West. This necessarily reduces the space between the two countries. In order to make him aware of the size of the heavy, thick, and crude absurdity into which he allowed himself to fall, I should like to ask our fancy talker how large the space could be between five and twenty degrees of latitude, for that is the distance between Peru and Mexico. They are at most three hundred fifty leagues from each other, so that it is a fool's wager to try to separate them by twelve hundred leagues. I wanted to decipher all this, [377r] in order to show the ignorance of the personage who, even if his calculations had not been false or erroneous, would not have won his case anyway, since it would have been a tenuous conclusion indeed to say that I meant to say that Gonzales Pizarro conquered Mexico, because he carried off some spoils from some Mexican lords.

### ERRONEOUS BOOKS

I see what the problem is, though, he is taking the position that all the conquests that the Spaniards effected in these countries were solely for booty, as those who produced a small book of the tyrannical and cruel actions of the Spaniards in the new world, and claim as author of this book my lord Brother Bartholomew de las Casas or Casaus, a Spanish Dominican, bishop of the royal city of Chiappa, and Jacques de Miggrode as translator. These are little tracts of falsehood, written by those who would never dare publish them under their own names, yet allow these untruths under the name of those who have traveled in those countries, in order to lend the weight of their names and authority to such rubbish.[9]

9.  Thevet's reference is to Bartolomé de las Casas's *Brevíssima relacíon de la destruycíon de las Indias*, translated into French by Jacques de Miggrode as *Tyrannies et cruautes des Espagnols, perpetrées és Indes Occidentales, qu'on dit le nouveau monde; brievement descrites en langue Castillane par l'Evesque Don Frere Bartelemy de Las Casas ou Casaus* (Antwerp, 1579). Thevet appears to be implying, here and in his reference to the "putative Las Casas" in the following paragraph, that the work is a forgery.

### THE EXAGGERATION OF THE CRUELTY
### OF THE SPANIARDS IN THE NEW WORLD

I could cite here, for instance, Girolamo Benzoni from Milan, who is cited as an eyewitness of the new world, but who never set foot there. He would have had a hard time crossing all those oceans, since, possibly, he never existed at all.[10] I prefer to turn him against our Spaniards whom these authors make such an effort to whitewash, since this putative Las Casas cites a certain Cacique,[11] to the effect that he would rather go to Hell than Heaven, where he had been told all the dead Spaniards went, in order that he might avoid the place where such cruel people would be. The Spaniards' cruelty is so exaggerated that it is alleged that they put more millions of men to death than there have been Spaniards since the beginning of time, and that they have devastated three times as much territory as all of Christendom.[12] I have not set out to excuse, palliate or disguise the great excesses which the Spaniards committed in the countries they discovered and conquered, since the facts would give me the lie, if I tried to pretend that they had always kept to the straight and narrow. But it is excessive to criticize them too harshly for that. Indeed, any man of sound judgment will agree with me, that natural law summons us to answer violence with force, since we see that the smallest animals try to take vengeance if one tries to hurt them, and hence the Spaniards, being among a fierce and rebellious people who had not learned to humble themselves under the yoke of his Catholic majesty found themselves obliged to use force to subdue those who kept a stiff neck and refused to obey the king.

10.   Benzoni not only existed but also spent the years from 1541 to 1557 in the New World. See Croizat's introduction to the Spanish edition of Benzoni's *Historia* by Gerulewicz, xxii–xxxi.

11.   This figure is identified as Hatuey in *Bartolomé de las Casas in History*, ed. Benjamin Keen and Juan Friede (DeKalb, 1971), 9.

12.   For more on the development of the "Black Legend" of Spanish atrocities against American Indians see Benjamin Keen, "The Black Legend Revisited: Assumptions and Realities," *Hispanic American Historical Review* 49 (1969):703–19, and Charles Gibson, ed., *The Black Legend: Anti-Spanish Attitudes in the Old World and the New* (New York, 1971).

## [377v] Force is necessary for conquest

All the conquests that the Romans and others effected were not tempered by any dim-witted facility. The reason is that, in order to legislate to foreigners, it was necessary to rely on feats of arms to obtain from these people, who never yield to gentleness, what they refused to grant of their own free will. Particularly if they were accustomed to being governed and ruled by a tyrant or by another who governed them badly and against their will. They have no wish to change their estate, out of fear of hopping from the frying pan into the fire. If they were not accustomed to obedience, and one tries to legislate for them, the desire imprinted on the heart of all men causes them to exceed the bounds of patience, when they find themselves forced to take some step outside the liberty to which they are accustomed. If, therefore, the Spaniards had to deal with unconquered people (as they did), who had never heard of the Law to which they were now subject, why are people upset because the Spaniards tickled [*chatouillé*] them a little harder than perhaps they might have wished?

## The good which the Spaniards did for the peoples of the New World

But, even if the Spaniards did mistreat these newly discovered people even more grievously, the good they did them compensated them for any harm they may have done. We all know that sodomy, idolatry and other forms of awful impiety were in fashion in this part of the world before the Spaniards set foot there. Today by the grace of God the light of Christianity, which arrived there because of them and through their ministry, has caused these pernicious corruptions (which were enough to condemn these poor Barbarians, who wallowed in these horrors, to the deepest regions of Hell) to be banished. When, therefore, we come to tote up the precise balance sheet of all the evil the Spaniards did in the new world with all the good they brought there, the accurate accounting will always show a profit against the difficulties and setbacks which the inhabitants received. I say this for the reader who is easy to persuade, not for those of a contrary turn of mind, who were unable to resist

harassing me with such speeches. Even when they grant that the
Spaniards did serve to lead these poor Barbarians to Christianity,
they insist that they did not have the right to use such violence.
Then, they mock what I say about Sodomy, idolatry, and other
desecrations being banished from the country by the arrival of the
Spaniards, for (as they say) they simply moved to new ground and
new inhabitants, after having exterminated those who were there
first [378r] and who were already subdued, or so oppressed them that
they could only breathe through Spanish lungs. That, though, is like
rendering judgment based on the bite of a flea (as we say), and is
ignoring the principle, particularly since, even if we were simply to
decide this matter, naturally, on the basis of purely human reason,
the cruelty to which these Barbarians subjected the poor Spaniards
was quite sufficient to embitter the latter. I know full well that these
people will say that, had the Spaniards not gone looking for truffles,
they would not have found them, but all will have to concede that
it is legitimate in natural law to show one's teeth to those who
would bite, and that the Barbarians made a serious mistake to have
been so cruel to the Spaniards, in view of the great good which
they were bringing them, far outweighing all the riches they might
have extracted from these lands, even though they be multiplied five
hundred million fold. These arguments will seem strange to the
uneducated who always insist that whatever somebody else does is
badly done while whatever they do, no matter how unsuitable, is the
best in the world.

### The voyage of Martin Forbisher [Frobisher]

I say this advisedly, since those who criticize the Spaniards so strongly
for their conquest of Peru, do not apply the same standards to the
discovery which they publish of Captain Martin Forbisher.[13]  As
if this Englishman would have ventured into such perils out of his
desire to bring this poor people to the Christian fold. He too was

13.   Several accounts of Frobisher's voyages were published in the late 1570s, but Thevet's
"Forbisher" suggests that he used *La navigation du capitaine Martin Forbisher anglois, és regions
de west & nordwest, en l'année M.D.LXXVII* (Geneva, 1578), a French translation by Nicolas
Pithou of *A True Report of the Last Voyage. . . .* (1577) by Dionyse Settle. Thevet's opinion
of this English Protestant is based on both religious and nationalistic antagonisms.

bitten, as experience has shown, by his lust for the treasures of this unknown country, which so fried his brains that he forgot his fear of all dangers to find the riches of the northern mines. Well do I know that they claim that the world is so perverted these days that no one would venture into these cold Northern seas were it not for the hope of profit. They claim further that God uses this avarice to befriend these poor Barbarians, to conquer them and bring them to reason and to civilization. What are the means towards this end? Are they other than musket shot and other acts of violence which they have decided to use against all rebellious and unconquered peoples? I am happy that this pleases them but, if they wish to accept the use of such means, they will be obligated to concede to the Spaniards that they had the right to beat these Barbarians, who were not only inflexible, but also very cruelly sacrificed many Christians to their Idols. If the Spaniards had been the first to dirty their hands in a conquered land, I would agree that it would be reasonable to criticize them. But they have such [378v] good clear models that it is self-evident that we cannot, save out of desperate malice, impute to cruelty the carnage which they made of these Barbarians, of whom it was better to rid the country than to allow them to roam the land, allowing them their execrable cruelties and their worship of their idols. Well and good, but where has the defense and protection of the Spaniards gotten us? It is time to withdraw, and bring to an end this encomium, which, without even realizing it, has grown to excessive proportions. The even-handed reader will be gracious enough to forgive this prolixity, and will believe that I let myself go this way in order to respond to the ceaseless cacophony of calumny of the name of the Spanish people, so that we might not again have to turn aside in order to answer these critics and nay-sayers, who seem to prefer that Godless Barbarism rather than Christianism reign yet over this part of the world. To hear them talk, though, you would think that the Barbarians had all the Humanity and Reformation they needed, in their dugouts. If their purpose is to denigrate the Spaniards, Pizarro and the others who explored Peru, they do not hesitate to embroider the truth, particularly since, if they wish to attack the Spaniard, they are obliged also to attack those whom they take such pleasure in defending. Since all they speak of is modesty and other equally delicate and courtly acts, I shall beg them to treat the Spaniards with the same kid gloves with which they handle their Forbisher who, because he refused to follow my advice, found himself in trouble from which he found it very difficult to escape.[14] But it is time I give up the hunt of these dim-wits, who spend all their time in their studies bemused by Platonic Ideas. If they ever had to act, they would find themselves in dire straits. They can cite their fallacious Benzoni all they wish, they will never carry the day, particularly with those with good sense and clear vision. I know well that they will attack me, that Pizarro was so base that he became a swineherd, as even Spanish historians say, but, if they were so gracious as to suspend their judgment and hear Pizarro's partisans out and draw their own conclusions, I am quite sure that they would not reduce this valiant warrior to such a low estate. Even if he was a poor commoner at the beginning, he nonetheless raised himself as high as a captain of his standing could aspire to.

14. We do not know what "advice" Thevet offered Frobisher, but the latter did have a copy of *Singularitez* in his ship's library. G. B. Parks, *Richard Hakluyt and the English Voyages* (New York, 1928), 46.

*FERDINAND CORTEZ, ESPAIGNOL.*

*Chapitre 55.*

IE seroie reputé fort mal courtois, si, descri-
uant les vies des hommes Illustres, ie laissoie
en arriere vn, qui de nom ne courtisoit pas
seulement les vertus, mais en tant qu'en luy
estoit les caressoit, & par heroïques, exploits
s'efuertuoit de s'approprier le plus qu'il luy e-
stoit possible l'effect du nõ, auquel il appro-
choit & se rendre courtois alẽdroit de ceux,
desquels la generosité & la vertu esmailloient tant en magnanimité
& prouesse qu'en pieté & doctrine. Le discours present seruira de

TTt iij

# Ferdinand Cortés,
# Spaniard

I should be held to be quite discourteous if, telling the life stories of famous men, I were to leave one out who not only courted virtue by virtue of his name but, in so far as it was in him, caressed virtues and by heroic exploits sought as much as he could to appropriate the effect of the name of courtesy[1] for himself, in which he was largely successful. He sought to be courteous toward those whose generosity and manly virtue shone as much in magnanimity and prowess as in piety and sound doctrine.

## Portrait of Ferdinand Cortés

The present discourse will serve [385v] as proof of all these points, and will furthermore make us admire the rarity of the perfections of this Spaniard, whose portrait I recovered from a Merchant of Seville when I was brought before the Inquisition on Saint Thomas's Day by some who tried to make us understand that we were Lutherans.[2] This good merchant delivered us from all danger after having conferred with me and recognized that he had seen me in Alexandria at the time of my trip to the Holy Land, of which I have already told you in my Cosmographie.[3] This good person led me to an office of his,

---

1. This is an elaborate and labored pun on Cortés's name and the Castilian word for *courtly.*

2. Thevet provided this interesting biographical detail in his *Cosmographie,* 2:f.491r. Also see Manuel Romero de Terreros, *Los retratos de Hernan Cortes* (Mexico, 1944), 23 and fig. 19.

3. This reference is to Thevet's first major work, *Cosmographie de Levant,* an account of his travels throughout the Middle East from approximately 1549 to 1553.

decorated with paintings and portraits of many travelers, of which he gave me several, including that of Cortés.

## NATIVITY AND PARENTS OF CORTÉS

He was born in 1485,[4] during the reign of Don Ferdinand and Lady Isabella of Aragon and Castille. His father was Martin Cortés de Monroi, son of Ferdinand Cortés, conqueror of Mexico.[5] His mother was Piçarro Altamirano. He was therefore the scion of four of the noblest families of the kingdom, to wit: the Cortés, Montroi, Piçarro and Altamirano. The families were not rich, but they were honored and respected by their neighbors, honor and respect that they worked hard to deserve.

## F. CORTÉS COMMISSIONED A LIEUTENANT

At a young age, he was commissioned an officer in a company of Genets [horse] for his cousin Alfonso de Hermosa, in the place of Captain Alfonso de Montroi, who wanted to make himself Master of his order against the wishes of the Queen, which caused Don Alfonso de Cardenas, master of Saint James [Santiago], to enter into overt hostilities against him. During this time our Cortés became ill, so much so that there seemed to be no more hope for him. His father, concerned that his health was suffering from too rigorous exercise, tried to withdraw him from military life and educate him instead.

## FERDINAND AT SCHOOL

For this reason, he [Cortés's father] sent him to study at Salamanca at the age of fourteen, where he spent two years learning grammar in the house of Francisco Nunnez de Valera, the husband of Martin Cortés's sister. Whether because the discipline was too tight, or

---

4. Much of the information in the next six paragraphs is taken, almost verbatim, from Gómara, *Historia de la conquista de Mexico*; we have used the English translation by Simpson, *Cortés*, 7–9. For an argument that Cortés was born in 1484 rather than 1485, see *Hernán Cortés*, ed. and trans. Pagden, xliii, n.14.

5. We take it that Thevet meant that Ferdinand was named for his grandfather.

because he was too short of money, or finally that he did not like the studious life, he returned to Medelin, where his father and mother, quite annoyed at his debauchery, laid him out in lavender *[luy lauerent la teste]*, as he deserved for having frustrated their plans for a noble life for him, had he deigned to pursue a career in the law.

### FERDINAND LEAVES THE LIBERAL ARTS, TO TAKE UP A MILITARY CAREER

But they failed to consider his nature was ill-suited to this subject, since it was impulsive, fiery, inconstant and suited to arms, so that any skill and nobility he might have was more likely to make itself felt in the martial [386r] arts and great enterprise than in deciding the law of a contentious case, whether by pen or tongue. Since he felt that his mother and father were little inclined to support a career in arms for him, he decided to leave and try his fortune elsewhere. Two circumstances intervened to aid the young warrior in his search, to wit: the conquest of Naples by Gonzales Hernandes de Cordova, known as the great captain,[6] and the expedition to the Indies of Nicolas de Ovando or Olanda, Commodore of Larez, who was sent by king Ferdinand as Viceroy to relieve Bombadilla [Francisco de Bobadilla]. He was torn as to which of the two to choose, but decided to go to the Indies, because Ovando knew him, and so would be more likely to take him on. In addition, the mountains of gold, which everybody knew were in the Indies, made him perk up his ears because of the heavy debts he claimed.

### CORTÉS'S TRIP TO THE INDIES POSTPONED BY THE FEVER

Just as he planned to join the fleet, which had been outfitted by Ovando, the onset of fever upset all his plans,[7] which angered him

---

6. Gonzales Fernández de Córdoba, "El Gran Capitán" (d. 1515), conquered Naples for Spain and improved the army through various measures. See Gerald de Gaury, *The Grand Captain: Gonzales de Cordoba* (London, 1955). Thevet included a chapter on Fernández de Córdoba in *Vrais pourtraits* (fols. 326–29).

7. Here Gómara tells a different story: "But, while Ovando was arranging his departure

enormously because of the loss of such a golden opportunity, which would not be likely to occur again. Nonetheless, he had no choice but to take heart and try to recover his health, then to search for another more auspicious opportunity. He was hardly out of bed when he set out for Italy, which he had earlier decided to forsake in favor of accompanying Ovando; in order to make it there, he set out for Valencia. The success of expeditions to the Indies made him want to catch the first breeze, no matter what it cost. After having wandered the countryside for a year, at the cost of inestimable pains and perils, he decided not to cross LA FLOR DEL BERRO[8] but to return with a view to going to the Indies after all. His mother and father could not dissuade him, though they reminded him of the difficulty of the trip, which might well claim his life, a life of which his country had great need. In the end, seeing that they were wasting their time, they gave him their blessing and money for the trip.

### CORTÉS'S DEPARTURE FOR THE INDIES

In his nineteenth year, and in our fifteen hundred and fourth, he made the passage to the Indies in a ship of Alonso Quintero, a native of Palos de Moguer, who took four other ships loaded with trade goods with him. Sailing Westward, Quintero raised the kingdoms of the Mexicans. Having rounded the last Cape of the Island of Cuba and leaving the islands Yucatan and Colhuacan on the left, where he had already earned a reputation for courtesy, Quintero arrived at the mouth of the great Panuco river. He heard there that this stream flowed from the mainland, and that it [386v] met the Vrabanes rivers in the interior and flowed from there to the North,

and the fleet was being readied, Cortés went to a house one night to visit a woman and, as he was walking along the badly cemented wall of the garden, it gave way with him. At the noise made by the falling wall and the arms and shield, a young husband, jealous of his wife, ran out and, seeing Cortés lying near the door, tried to kill him, but was prevented from doing so by his old mother-in-law. Cortés was injured by the fall, and besides was stricken with a quartan fever, which kept him in bed for a long time, so he was unable to go with governor Ovando" (Gómara, *Cortés*, 8–9). Gómara also wrote that Cortés was "much given to consorting with women, and always gave himself to them" (409).

8.   We have been unable to identify this reference. Our use of small capital letters follows Thevet's text.

toward the country of Bacchalaura.[9] Quintèro had not been hanging around the coast long before he heard from two interpreters from the islands of Yucatan and Colhuacan that the kingdoms of the Mexicans spread west from there, and that they were rich in painters, masons, and other skilled workers. That pricked Fernand's[10] interest, who promptly tried to master the situation and tried to win the hearts of the Mexicans with sweetness and courtesy. He was in fact so gracious to them that they thought he was not Spanish, but they could not see any further than the ends of their noses. They learned later at their own expense how he kept himself warm at night; he did not in fact tarry in starting the lesson.

## CORTÉS'S SUCCOR OF A MEXICAN PRINCE

He heard that those peoples were quarreling over the boundaries between their territories; when a neighbor, lord of this land, asked for help against his enemies, Cortés did not wait to be asked a second time. Cortés allied himself with this prince very much to his own advantage, for he was fully aware that this poor prince, so hard pressed from all sides that he did not know to which saint he should pray, would consider himself very fortunate to have any support at all from Cortés, who had at his disposal a company of musketeers, archers and pikemen with a squad of mounted men-at-arms, a formidable force to these poor Barbarians. On the day of the battle [of Cholula?], Fernand arranged his men so as to make one great charge, though they were but few in number. He let the cannons fire and the horses whinny; the enemies were so terrified by the roar of these thundering cannons that, after losing many of their men, they proclaimed themselves defeated and surrendered. The lord [Cortés's ally] did not at first wish to accept the surrender, because of the custom he had of refusing mercy to those who had once rebelled against him. When Cortés urged him to show mercy, however, he did so solely out of respect for the Spaniard, whom he knew to be primarily responsible for his victory. After this expedition Ferdinand, full of confidence in his men and in the means at his

9. Cf. Giovio's biography of Cortés in *Gli elogi vite brevemente*, f.314r.
10. Thevet switches arbitrarily between Fernand, Ferdinand, and Ferrand.

disposal to affect his will, began to attack Mutezuma or Motzume, or even Montzum, who, because of the power he wielded in this country, was not pleased to see Christians in it. Montezuma was nobody's fool, and knew full well that the Christians had designs on the kingdom and sovereignty of Mexico, so he began to treat with a vassal of his to exterminate them.

### MONTEZUMA, KING OF THE MEXICANS, AGAINST THE SPANIARDS

He was, however, trying to act too rashly, because [387r] *Qualpopaca*, Prince of Nanthlan or, according to others, Naucutel, later named Almerie, put nine Christians to death. Fernand took full advantage of the situation and, to exact vengeance, put into effect the plan he had dreamed of but had never been able to execute for lack of an adequate pretext, that of attacking Montezuma directly. The murder of these nine opened such a broad avenue for Fernand's attack that all Montezuma's vast army could not stand against the wounds they received from Spanish swords and the thunder of Cortés's artillery, which blasted Montezuma's poor soldiers and left the remainder vulnerable to Spanish swords. It was a terrible slaughter, which terrified the Mexicans, who thought that the men at arms were Centaurs,[11] and that the Christians made thunder come down from the sky by virtue of some special favor they enjoyed with Jupiter; they found no alternative to surrender.

### THE KING OF THE MEXICANS IS CONQUERED

Montezuma himself surrendered, and delivered all the people of his empire to Cortés's will. Later on, however, because of rumors of a rebellion which he was fostering with some of his countrymen, he was put in irons. This so enraged the pagans that they all ran to the place where he was sitting in chains, whether because they wanted to liberate him from the indignity to which was being subjected the greatest and most powerful man they had known, or because they

---

11. There are numerous references in the sources to the natives' belief that Spaniards mounted on horses were centaurs. For examples see Gómara, *Cortés*, 46, 50, 69, and Giovio, *Gli elogi vite brevemente*, f.315v.

were furious that he had given up to Cortés, they threw a multitude of great rocks at their king.

## DEATH OF MONTEZUMA

Even though the Spaniards did their best to chase the Mexicans away, the former were not able to prevent a rock from striking him in the head and killing him.[12] In his place the Mexicans elected Qualttimoc [Cuauhtémoc], or perhaps *Cuctravacin*, Montezuma's brother and prince of Istapalipa.[13]

## CORTÉS SUBSTITUTED FOR MONTEZUMA,
### BUT REFUSES THE TITLE

On the Spaniards' side, on the other hand, most of the nobles held Cortés to be Montezuma's successor, which freed him to pursue his rival for Montezuma's throne by fire and sword: even though he had been elected King, he refused this title, contenting himself with that of Vice-Roy.[14]

## CORTÉS DEFEATS NARVAEZ

It was however much easier for him to conquer the new king than it had been to defeat Montezuma, because he claimed to have defeated Captain Narvaez in the meantime. Narvaez had arrived in the city of Veracruz with a company of nine hundred soldiers with a commission from Diego Velasquez, Governor of Cuba, to kill Cortés or to chase him from the country by force of arms, because he had not reported to Velasquez on his expedition and the territory he had

12.   There are two divergent versions of Montezuma's death. The first, given by Cortés himself, other Spanish sources, and here repeated by Thevet, is that the natives stoned the king to death. A second version, that Montezuma was stabbed to death shortly before the Spaniards left the city, is advanced by native writers. For details, see *Hernán Cortés*, ed. and trans. Pagden, 477–78, n.89.

13.   Gómara called Cuauhtémoc a nephew of Montezuma (*Cortés*, 239).

14.   Cortés was governor, justicia mayor, and captain-general but not viceroy. Thevet apparently copied this error from Giovio, who says the same thing (*Gli elogi vite brevemente*, f.316r).

discovered.[15] While Cortés was occupied with defeating Narvaez, he found the Mexicans completely changed. Having armed themselves, they had made a terrible massacre of the Spaniards whom he had left as a garrison in Mexico under [387v] his lieutenant Captain Pedro d'Alvarado; they chased Cortés from the city where he thought to rest after all his troubles and travails.

### Cortés's siege of Themistitan

He had to start all over and, in 1521, with the help of the Spaniards he brought back from his victory over Narvaez, he placed the city of Themistitan under siege. The siege lasted three months, at the end of which he entered the city. He and his men were nonetheless bested by those Mexicans. Seeing no hope of successful resistance, they [the natives] knew full well that the determination of the Spaniards was fueled solely by their lust for the gold and precious stones with which such an opulent city was decorated. For this reason, they gathered all the gold and silver they had, and threw it into the city's lakes. All the Spaniards found were empty mountings, which so enraged them that there was no torture to which they did not subject these miserable people. Cortés himself was the most bewildered by the fact that, having searched everywhere, he was unable to find neither Montezuma's treasure nor trace of the gold or silver which he had left in the city when he fled.

### Torture of Qualttimoc and his secretary

Seeing that he was unable to draw from any of them where they had hidden their treasures, even though he threatened them with worse than the punishment with which he had rewarded *Qualpopaca's* cruelty (whom he had burned), he had the king *Qualttimoc* and his secretary put to such severe torture that there was not a bone, muscle or tendon in their poor bodies which had not suffered

15.   After serving in Jamaica, Pánfilo de Narváez helped Diego de Valásquez conquer Cuba. In 1520, Velásquez sent him to Mexico to force Cortés into submission. Narváez's force was defeated, however, and he was captured and imprisoned. After his release in 1521, he returned to Spain, where Charles V commissioned him *adelantado* to conquer and settle Florida. After a futile search for gold there, Narváez died on his way to Mexico in 1528.

a forced conversion.[16] He thought to gain by force what he could not by orders or threats, but he was unable to draw a word of their secret from them.

## Death of the secretary

They say that the secretary was so courageous that, even while the Spaniards were roasting him over a slow fire, all he wanted to talk about was the evil of the Spaniards; he died at the end of six hours at the hands of his torturers.

## Death of the king of Mexico

Cortés saw that the king was no more inclined to talk, so he gave up on torturing him, but led him about the provinces bound and gagged, then had him hanged.[17] When he had thus disposed of this enemy, he started to search anew, because he had heard that Mexico was so rich in gold and treasures that it would awaken the most cowardly person one could imagine to yet greater feats, to increase the renown of such deeds and magnanimous conquests. If the report of his expeditions is accurate, this is perforce the person who [388r] comes second in conditions and qualities to none of the other Conquerors. You have heard the tricks, courtesies, and brave exploits with which he prosecuted these Indians, (even though if one examined the matter carefully, as we shall show in the life of Montezuma, there are certain extremes quite unsuitable to the Christian piety of a heroic warrior), by which they became wiser as well as sadder. I shall now treat the other expeditions which he made through several seas in order to render his name yet more illustrious. I shall not take the space to talk of his discovery of the great, snow-capped mountain which threw flame and burning stones to its base in the manner of Mount

---

16. A pun: which had not been turned back on itself.

17. According to Benzoni (*History of the New World*, ed. Smyth, 138), Cortés seized the king and his secretary and tortured both: "the secretary was most cruelly burnt by slow degrees, he all the time exclaiming severely—*con grandissima lamentatione*—against the wickedness of the Christians, and died in six hours." Cuauhtémoc, however, did not die under torture but was hanged four years later during the Honduran expedition for allegedly plotting a rebellion against Cortés.

Etna in Sicily, not because I am caving in to the stubbornness of those scowling skeptics who refuse to believe anything unless the evidence for it hits them in the eye, but rather because I am not sufficiently convinced by my sources to vouch for its authenticity myself.[18] In order to praise our Ferrand, it will be much more fitting that I make much of his true piety toward the church of God, which caused him to conquer and subject to the Christian faith most of the peoples whom he vanquished and subjected to the rule of the Emperor Charles V.

## ERROR OF PAUL IOVE [PAOLO GIOVIO]

I am not doing this because I seek to do the same sort of thing as Paul Iove, who, because of Cortés's punctiliousness at the sacraments, a punctiliousness that a few overbold historians have pointed out resembled witchcraft by the twelve Apostles, showed him at his prayers as if he were a homebody instead of a gallant and hardy pioneer. No, his Zeal for the glory of God caused him to lead to the slaughter-house of Jesus Christ the lost sheep who had been prey to the fangs of ravaging lions and wolves.

## MEXICAN AMBASSADORS TO THE EMPEROR AND THE POPE

He made them so thoroughly Christian that two of the most illustrious Mexican nobles were sent as ambassadors to pay their respects to the Emperor in Spain and to Pope Clement in Rome, each of whom gave them the warmest welcome imaginable. Cortés built a sumptuous mansion at Themistitan in the form of a royal palace, enriched with marble and carved stone, which many Spaniards say is more beautiful than the Al[h]ambra of Granada because the stones of different colors are so well integrated into the design. He certainly had the wherewithal to build it from his rich booty.

---

18.   Thevet appears to be criticizing Gómara and Giovio, who both compared Popocatépetl to Mount Etna in Sicily (*Cortés*, 131–32; *Gli elogi vite brevemente*, f.316r).

## Cortés's rich booty

Among others, I have found that he has, in Castille, five emeralds set in gold worth one hundred thousand écus: one made into a rose with [388v] its leaves; another like a horn; the third in the form of a fish; the fourth, like a bell of which the clapper is a great pearl in the form of a pear; and the fifth into a cup, for which alone a Genevan jeweler offered forty thousand ducats in the hope of selling it for even more.

## Cortés's recall to Spain

Cortés's sudden riches exposed him to envy, which never leaves those who do well. He got much the same treatment that Columbus had: he was recalled to Spain, where he brought rich and precious presents for the Emperor, who gave him the city of Gallio[19] as a reward, to him and his descendants. His successor, sent to Mexico with plenipotentiary authority, was Don Antonio de Mendozza, the son of the Count of Tendilla. In this way, Ferdinand, who had first conquered Mexico and subjected it to the Emperor Charles V, was deprived of the fruits of his labors and perils.[20] He nonetheless continued to exhibit the same praiseworthy zeal he had always shown in the imperial service.

## Cortés in Africa with Charles V

He followed the Emperor to Africa, where he lost many of his most valuable furnishings in the loss of Algiers. Seven years later, he died in his house, but not at a very old age, to the great regret of all those who love *virtù*, and who ought to cherish those who try to become illustrious in its service.

## Cortés's death

It would have given me pleasure to honor Cortés, whose eyes lit

19. Thevet's error ultimately derives from Giovio's phrase "la terra di Vallio," a reference to Cortés's title Marques del Valle del Oaxaca (*Gli elogi vite brevemente*, ff. 317–18).

20. Cortés's own complaints are made in his Fifth Letter; see *Hernán Cortés*, ed. and trans. Pagden, 442–44.

the world, by including an anthology of the epitaphs written in his
honor, but I shall limit myself to the following one in Italian:

> Great Hercules of old, did mighty things
> and overcame at last his sufferings.
> But Fernando second unto none,
> by nobler acts has Hercules outdone.
> Cortés a greater traveler than he
> though not so strong, has compassed land and sea.
> Made the Antipodes obey his nod;
> And what is more, acknowledge one true god.[21]

21. Translation from the Italian in *Prosopographia* (1676 ed., 78). The epitaph, by
Franchino da Cosenza, is in Giovio, *Gli elogi vite brevemente*, f.318: Thevet apparently
copied the part of the poem on f.318r, but not the remainder on 318v.: "Bacchus, having
subdued the black Eoans,/ From them he turned the honors due to God./ But this the
good Hernando did not do, after/ He had conquered the other India, to which he was
compassionate;/ Thus the great Cortes was of more importance to us/ Than Bacchus was
to the wicked age;/ The latter did not wish to be called God,/ While the former had himself
worshipped by force."

ALPHONSE ALBVQVERQVE.

*Chapitre 66.*

I la prolixité ne me degouſtoit ie prendroie
plaiſir de faire marcher d'vn meſmes dacty-
le auec ce Capitaine Portugais Vaſque de
Gama, Edoüard Pacheco & autres guer-
riers, qui pour le ſeruice de la Courōne Por-
tugaiſe ont fait retétir le bruit de leur renō-
mée par les endroits de ces contrées inco-
gneuës. Ie ſuis contraint m'arreſter à ceſtuy
ſeul, lequel, par ſes valeureux exploicts, a merité d'eſtre cōparé auec
les plus grands Capitaines, dont la memoire eſt celebrée par les Hi-

# Alfonso d'Albuquerque

If verbosity did not disgust me, I would be happy to write in the same style as that Portuguese captain Vasco de Gama, Edward Pacheco and other warriors who, for the benefit of the Portuguese crown, have trumpeted their renown throughout these unknown lands.[1] I am constrained to pause only over he who, by his valorous exploits, has earned the right to be compared with the greatest captains, whose memory is made famous by [420v] Historians.[2]

## Summary of Albuquerque's mores

He has acquired the reputation of having been a great judge, very severe toward perjurers, a righter of wrongs against one and all, and of chaste conversation.[3] He never married, and had but one son by a servant.[4] He worked harder than any, to the point that he overburdened those who worked with him but, to encourage them, instead of threats, he would put his own back into the task. Slanderers were not welcome around him, so that a heap of tale

1. Vasco de Gama wrote nothing himself, but Portuguese chroniclers wrote at length about his voyages. Duarte Pacheco Pereira wrote a guide to West African navigation, *Esmeraldo de situ orbis*, that was well known to seamen in Thevet's time, although it was not published until 1892.

2. For a discussion of the literature, see Donald F. Lach, *Asia in the Making of Europe*, 2 vols. (Chicago, 1965–77), 1, bk. 1:181–98, and 2, bk. 2:138–49.

3. Much of Thevet's information in this chapter, including this section on Albuquerque's *Mores*, comes from *Histoire de Portugal*, ed. and trans. Goulart, a French translation of Jeronimo Osorio's *De rebus Emmanuelis gestis* (Lisbon, 1571) and additional materials on Portuguese discoveries by Fernão Lopes de Castanheda and others. Thevet mentions Goulart's work in the text.

4. Albuquerque's illegitimate son Brás (later called Alfonso) wrote *Commentarios de Afonso Dalboquerque*.

carriers, who usually cluster around leaders' ears, did not dare to make false accusations (on penalty of repenting of it). His plans were always carefully thought out with incredible diligence to carry out his designs. He loved truth and hated falsehood. In short, he was one of the most accomplished and perfect Captains of whom we have ever heard. In order to show you that I do not invent this praise out of thin air, let us see in detail his conduct in carrying out the responsibilities entrusted to him.

### FRANCISCO ALBUQUERQUE, BROTHER OF ALFONSO

I shall pass quickly over the evidence he gave both of wisdom and of prowess in his own country, to send him to the Indies, whither he was dispatched with his brother Francisco by Emanuel, King of Portugal in the year 1504.[5] Not for long, though, did he have the company of his brother, who worked wonders there: indeed, he had crushed the pride of these Indians, both by his generosity toward Trimumpara, the King of Cochim [Cochin], and by the victories which he [Francisco] won over the Calecutians, whose King was forced to accede to the peace which it pleased the Portuguese to dictate.[6] Contrary to the peace, Juan Fernand Correa attacked a vessel carrying pepper belonging to the King of Calecut [Kozhikode] which was making for Cranganor, and even though Naubeadarim[7] complained to Francisco Albuquerque about this attack, he was unable to move him to make good on his losses. This caused the King of Calecut to take up arms, and he attacked Albuquerque's men so hard that they had no choice but to show their backs, and to leave the hapless King of Cochim in a mess. Meanwhile, they sent to the King to ask

5.   This sentence contains two errors copied from *Histoire de Portugal*, ed. and trans. Goulart, 103. Francisco de Albuquerque was Alfonso's cousin, and they sailed for India in 1503.

6.   The Hindu ruler of Cochin had established commercial relations with the Portuguese in 1502. When the Albuquerques arrived, he had been driven to take refuge on the island of Vaipim (in the Indian Ocean?). Franciso de Albuquerque restored him to power.

7.   According to *Histoire de Portugal*, ed. and trans. Goulart, 91, Naubeadarim was "son of the sister of the King of Calicut and, according to the laws of his country, the sole pretender to the throne." Brás de Albuquerque states that he was the principal governor of Coulão (*Commentarios*, ed. Birch, 1:8–9).

him for reinforcements, but he refused. They left for Portugal, with dire consequences; in this retreat this Francisco and Nicholas Coeillo [Coelho], with all those in their squadron were plunged so far out to sea that they have never since felt like bringing back news of where they had been.

## EXPEDITION OF ALBUQUERQUE
### THE KINGDOM OF ORMUS [HORMUZ]

After this loss Alfonso never lost heart, but undertook yet greater enterprises; for instance he cast covetous eyes on the kingdom of Ormus, in order to seize control of it, accompanied by six valiant and famous Officers, to wit Francisco Tavore, Manuel Tellio, Alfonso Lopez de Coste, Nonio Vasque de Blanc Castel, [421r] Anthony de Cam[p] and John Nonio, who commanded 470 soldiers.[8] At Curiate [Kuryat], Mascate [Muscat] and Orfazam [Orfaçaom], the largest cities of the kingdom of Ormus, the force of their bravery and daring was felt to the point that they reduced the King so that he had to pretend to wish to enter into negotiations under the terms dictated by Albuquerque, unless he submitted to these conditions in order to lead the Portuguese into a trap, one he tried without success to spring, for the loss of several of his Lieutenants and ships plunged him into such despair that he had to beg for peace again with a rope around his neck: so Zerzadim [Ceifadin] II, the King of Ormus, promised to be the vassal of King Emmanuel, and to give him fifteen thousand ducats a year in tribute, and five thousand the first year to Albuquerque for the expenses of the war. He was also required to assign a place to build a citadel, at Albuquerque's choice, of which the foundations were immediately put into place. Albuquerque, familiar with the Sarrasins' [Saracens'] mood, had a tower built on an isthmus near the sea and the site of his citadel, where he placed several cannons, in order to discourage any who might wish to stop him in his enterprise.

8.  Thevet refers here to Francisco de Tavora, Manuel Teles, Afonso Lopes da Costa, Nuño Vaz de Castelo-branco, Antonio do Campo, and João da Nova.

### Conspiracy against Albuquerque

At the beginning, the officers and soldiers outdid each other in working on building the fort but, because the task dragged on too long, some of the Portuguese began to tire, and conspired against him: they caused it to be known by means of Cojetar,[9] first counselor of the King of Ormus, that Albuquerque did not have instructions from the King of Portugal to build a citadel, and they hatched a plot in secret to slow Albuquerque's plans, but it was discovered by a Moor, named Abraham, which caused Albuquerque to prepare for war.

### Albuquerque's cruelty toward some of his enemies

Zerzadim, knowing that his snare was uncovered, began to work out in the open: for his part Albuquerque prepared so carefully that he seized several barques that Cojetar had ordered to call at the port, and there he committed an act unworthy of his valorous exploits: he had the nostrils, ears and the hands cut off the archers and boatmen and, as for the others, he split one foot in the middle in addition. Then he had them put ashore, telling them to go tell Cojetar that anybody who undertook to deliver victuals to the city of Ormus would suffer like treatment. To tell the truth, had he not been abandoned by Manuel Tellio, Alfonso Lopés de Coste and Anthony de Camp,[10] he would have carried the day. As it was, in the retreat, he still took Arbez and Homeal, which is on the island named Queixumes, and forgot no [421v] act of hostility. I am ashamed to say what he did at Calajate [Kalyat], since it will appear that all I wish to do here is list his atrocities. As Zafaradin, followed by a great troop of Indians, sought to take Albuquerque and his men unawares, he and his men were surrounded by the Portuguese and, since Albuquerque was angry at this race, he once again had the noses and ears cut off all his prisoners, and burned the city, the magnificent temple, and twenty-seven ships in the harbor.

---

9.   Cojeatar (Kwaja Atar) ruled Ormuz on behalf of King Ceifadim, who was fifteen years old.

10.   These three, along with Francisco de Tavora, led the mutiny referred to above.

## BAD BLOOD BETWEEN ALBUQUERQUE
## AND FERNAND COUTIN [COUTINHO]

After the recall by King Emanuel of Francisco Almeida to Portugal, Albuquerque had a set-to with Fernand Coutin, a very well-known Gentleman and Field Marshal of the Kingdom: for, even though this Coutin was only charged with making known Albuquerque's possession of the government of Ormus, they found themselves so at loggerheads that the Portuguese interests very nearly suffered from the strife between the two of them.    Coutin, seeing Albuquerque win the victory over the Calecutians of which he had counted on the honor for himself, puffed up with pride conceived a great hatred for Albuquerque, whom he would have wished more cowardly, so that he could have gained the glory of having avenged the death of Lawrence Almeida on these Calecutians.[11] I shall not dwell on the high opinion we should have of Albuquerque's prowess, in order to praise his patience as the victorious governor of Ormus at putting up with the outrageous tricks of this arrogant Coutin, who finally learned to his sorrow by the unhappy outcome whether the game of constantly putting himself forth was worth the candle. In fact he was killed by the Calecutians with Manuel Pazagne and Vasque de Sylveire, who ended up as trophies for their enemies, because they struck out on their own and did not follow Albuquerque.


## ALBUQUERQUE VICE-ROY IN THE INDIES,
## HIS EXPLOITS AT GOA

The latter, installed as Vice-Roy in India[12] for his King in Portugal, rolled up his sleeves. God knows what exploits he performed at Goa against Zabarim [Zabaim] Dalcam, prince of that Isle, of which he finally made himself Master, on the sixteenth of February in the year of our Lord 1510, which he ruled wisely and as well as he could, trying above all to repress the insolence of the soldiers and to gain the amity of all the inhabitants and their neighbors, but his men

11.    Lourenço de Almeida died in a naval battle with an Egyptian fleet in the Indian Ocean in 1508.

12.    Although Albuquerque was governor of India, he was never viceroy; *Histoire de Portugal*, ed. and trans. Goulart, makes no such claim.

caused him much grief by their disunity. They had even gathered to dethrone him, as they would have done, if he had not surprised them in the house where they thought themselves safe, most of whom he dismissed, while forgiving the others. They nonetheless continued to deceive him and, conspiring with Zabarim, threw him off the Isle of Goa where thereafter, however he played his cards, he still found himself tangled up with Zabaim, [422r] whom he actually gave a lot of trouble and broke up much of his state,

### Death of Anthony Norogne
### [Antonio de Noronha]

but he suffered a great loss in the death of Anthony Norogne, his nephew, who, as he boarded Zufalarim's ship,[13] as he stepped on the bridge, had his left thigh [knee] pierced by an arrow loosed from the walls of Goa, from which blow he died in three days, to the great sorrow of his men. Zabaim was finally successful at capturing Goa at sword's point. Albuquerque never lost sight of his goal, to assure Portuguese interests not just for a few years, as Almeida had done, but to lay a firm foundation for their domination, which he was sure must last long into the future.[14]

### Albuquerque the founder of Portuguese
### dominion over the Indies

Hence it is that several have justly written that he was the founder of Portuguese domination in India, as my lord [Simon] Goulart has quite rightly noted in the History of Portugal which he communicated to us French. He did not content himself with having conquered the country but, in so far as it was in him, tried to make such a mixture that he coupled the Portuguese with Indian women, so that India might be repeopled by Portuguese: to this end he married Portuguese soldiers with the women of the country, calling the soldiers his sons

---

13. Zufularim was characterized as the "valiant captain" of a ship under Zabaim Dulcan. Ibid., 256.

14. Thevet took this comparison directly from ibid., 271–72.

and the women his daughters-in-law, whom he invited to his house, giving various presents to their husbands.

## ALBUQUERQUE'S SUCCESS AT MALACA

At Malaca he was no less successful than at Goa and, even though at the beginning he took no special notice of the summons of Diego Mendoz of Vasconcel,[15] still he leveled the power of the King of Malaca, with his great and terrible elephants and, after he was able to land in Malaca, ruled the city by good laws and ordinances, and had a Citadel built there, using as his building materials the tombs of the Kings and Princes, the stones of the most beautiful buildings of the city, reduced to ruins by cannons during the war. For governor and judge of the Mohammedans, he chose Vretimutaraja [Utimata Raja], and Ninachetuen [Nina chatu] for the other races, those who served other idols. Now, ambition so blinded this Vretimuraia that he showed no scruples at surveying the Malacan kingdom to the prejudice of his King, perhaps because he was relying on his great wealth, or on the good will of Albuquerque, a close relation,[16] or on his own skill to bring his designs to fruition.

## EXECUTION OF VRETIMORAIA, GOVERNOR
### OF MALACA, BECAUSE OF HIS BEHAVIOR

But he was quite far off the mark, for as soon as Albuquerque had uncovered this treachery, he did not rest until he had cut off the heads of his son, his son-in-law and others who had helped in this conspiracy. This is how the great must hold the scales of justice, without allowing them to tilt to one side or the other. He was the special enemy of tyranny, and punished severely those who discharged [422v] the public trust to which they were called badly. He showed this all the more clearly to Patecatir, Vretimuraia's deputy. This poor unfortunate allowed himself to be so taken in by the

15. Diego Mendes de Vasconcellos arrived in India in 1510 with orders to conquer Malacca and govern it independently from Albuquerque.

16. Albuquerque and Utimata Raja, of course, were not related by blood. Thevet may simply mean they were allies, as was reported in *Histoire de Portugal*, ed. and trans. Goulart, 298.

widow, who gave him her daughter whom he wanted very much in marriage, that he wished to rise against the Portuguese. But Albuquerque repressed this foolhardy man so cleverly that he wised up in a few days [*qu'en peu de iours il deuint sage à ses despens*], and remained quiet, giving no more trouble to anyone.[17]

## ALBUQUERQUE'S EXPLOITS IN ARABIA

In Arabia he did wondrous things as well and, even though he was forced to raise the siege of Aden, he was still honored by Melichias[18] and others from that area. This story would never end if we recounted each instance of his diligence and zeal to assure, as completely as it was in him to do, the authority of his Prince, in the Indies and particularly at Ormus. And because in my tale of this island I would like, if I may, to say a little more, I shall close this discourse with the disease that, aided by his old age, came to seize him by the scruff of the neck.[19]

## PEDRO ALBUQUERQUE

So, feeling the end approach, he commissioned Pedro Albuquerque, whose virtue and qualities he knew from experience and whom he knew to be well regarded both by the King and by the people, Governor of Ormus.[20] For this reason, he recommended him to the King of Ormus. What put him in his grave was the message he received from Cide Hali and an Ambassador of the King of Persia that Loup Soarez had been sent by Emanuel to be Vice-Roy.[21] They found this

17.   In fact, Patecatir waged war against the Portuguese but was defeated and forced to flee to Java. Ibid., 303–5.

18.   Melichiz was governor of Diu. Ibid., 196.

19.   Thevet never does discuss the disease, dysentary, that killed Albuquerque in December 1515 at the age of sixty-two.

20.   The exploits of Pero de Albuquerque are recounted in Brás de Albuquerque's *Commentarios*, ed. Birch, 4:108–21, 188–92. Brás called him Afonso's nephew, but Sanceau said he was a "young cousin." *Indies Adventure*, 293.

21.   Thevet's Cide Hali, taken from *Histoire de Portugal*, ed. and trans. Goulart, 385, may be Hasan Ali. Sanceau, *Indies Adventure*, 294. Lopes Soares de Albergaria was the third Portuguese governor of India, replacing Albuquerque. He "aspired to be Governor of India purely in order

They found this unjust and unreasonable, and offered him their support if he wished to stay, to hunt those who wanted to overthrow him. Albuquerque thanked them, preferring to be low and humble to earning the anger and hatred of his King to whom he wrote before dying, in the year 1515, to recommend his son whom he was leaving.[22]

## Death of Albuquerque

The news of his death saddened not only the King of Portugal, but also afflicted several other Princes, among others Xuxanda [Xuranda], King of Ormus, who wept warm tears and wore mourning. As for the King of Portugal, he was extremely sorry, and sent for the son of Albuquerque, named Blaise, to whom he gave the name of his father, commanding that he be henceforth called Alfonso, in order that the name of so great a man might not die. Then he gave great gifts to this son, and married him to a great lady.

to gratify his vanity and satisfy a petty spite, for Lopo Soares hated Albuquerque for reasons not on record." Ibid., 255.

22.   Albuquerque's letter is in *Histoire de Portugal*, ed. and trans. Goulart, 386, and is translated into English in Prestage, *Afonso de Albuquerque*, 63–64, and Sanceau, *Indies Adventure*, 296.

# CHRISTOFLE COLOMB, GENEVOIS
### Chapitre 100.

E dire commun, qui porte que ceux, qui
promettent des montaignes d'or, font eſtat
de choſe, qui ne ſe peut accomplir, ſe trou-
uera eclipſé par la recerche diligente de ceſt
excellent pilote, lequel ayant promis aux
Roys d'Angleterre, Portugal & d'Eſpaigne
telles montaignes, par effeçt les exhiba à ce-
luy qui voulut croire le ſage conſeil de ce
Capitaine Geneuois, ſur le nom duquel certains ont voulu plus gail-
lardement que prudemment, & à propos ſubtiliſer, quant faiſans

# CHRISTOPHER COLUMBUS, GENOESE

The commonplace that those who promise mountains of gold make promises they cannot keep is given the lie by the diligent search of this excellent navigator. Having promised such rich mountains to the kings of England, Portugal and Spain, he delivered them to the king who had faith in his good advice.

## DARING COMPARISON OF COLUMBUS WITH NOAH'S DOVE

Some wags have made puns that were more daring than prudent on the relationship between his name and the dove which brought [522v] news of the sighting of land back to Noah's Ark, saying that Columbus flew so high that he found land which had been unknown to us.[1] Without trying to follow such sophisticated humor, we shall do our best to represent as succinctly as possible the life of him whose portrait, which I found at Lisbon along with several others as I have said elsewhere, graces these pages.

## COLUMBUS'S BIRTHPLACE

He was a native of Cuguero or, as some say, of Albizolo, a mean little village on the Gennes [Genoa] river, near to Savonna.[2]

1. *Colomb* in French means dove. Ferdinand Columbus, who wrote a biography of his father in the 1530s (published in Venice in 1571), is one of the authors who pointed out this meaning of Columbus's name. See *The Life of the Admiral*, ed. and trans. Keen, 4.

2. These place-names are mentioned in several of Thevet's sources in a variety of combinations. Albissola (Thevet's Albizolo), however, is mentioned only by Paolo Giovio, in the form "Arbizolo," and he described it as a "villa aspra, & ignobile della riviera di Genoa appresso

### Observation which moved Columbus to the discovery of the New World

While Columbus was plying his trade in Portugal and passing through the straits of Gibraltar, he had noticed from long experience that, at certain times of the year, there were Easterly winds which lasted several days on end, without varying at all. Convinced that these winds had to come from land, he formed such a strong idea in his mind of this land across the sea that he ended up deciding to find it.

### Columbus urges the Genoans to give him the means to discover the New World

According to Urbain Chauveton in his history of the new world, as recounted by Peter Martyr of Milan, he presented himself to the Signoria of Genoa at the age of approximately forty, and proposed his plan to pass through the straits of Gibraltar and sail so far on the Eastern sea that, going completely around the world, he would end up at the lands that produced spices. He promised to obligate himself to complete the voyage, on the condition that he be provided with a few ships victualed and fitted out. The enterprise seemed perilous in the extreme, but taking short cuts was out of the question.[3] For this reason, he decided to try his luck elsewhere, and went to Portugal, where he found King Alfonso V preoccupied with his ventures in Africa and the exploitation of Oriental trade, and to Castille, where he found the king occupied with his campaign in Granada.

### Bartholomew in England

At that point, he sent his brother Bartholomew to Henry VII of England who, even though he was rich and was not encumbered by any war, chickened out [*saigna du nés*] like the rest of them and sent Bartholomew packing without giving him anything.

Savona." *Gli elogi vite brevemente*, f.174r.

3.    The story of Columbus asking the Republic of Genoa for aid was told first in Ramusio, *Terzo volume delle navigationi*, f.1r, and was later repeated by Benzoni, in *History of the New World*, ed. and trans. Smyth, 16. Ramusio claimed Peter Martyr as his authority for this assertion, but we have found no such statement in Martyr's works.

## Columbus refused by the king of Portugal

Having failed in this mission, he began to treat of this undertaking with the king of Portugal, who gave him as cold a welcome as the English and the Genoans had done. Roderic, the bishop of Viso [Viseu], and several other frightening types at the Portuguese court claimed to be experts in cosmography, and treated the hapless Genoan to a blistering welcome, in which they stated categorically that there were not and could not be gold nor riches in the West as Columbus was asserting.[4] Columbus discovered that he had acquired the reputation [523r] among the Genoans of a liar, among the English of a crazy man who amused the assembled throngs, and among the Portuguese of a dreamer without many brains. These insults did not make Columbus lose heart, though–they merely made him sail to Paly [Palos] de Moguer, where he unburdened himself to Juan Perez, Cordelier de la Rúbida [Rábida], a well regarded Cosmographer.[5] Perez advised him to talk his plan over with Henry, Duke of Medine Sidonia and then with Luis, Duke of Medine Celi, but they gave no more than the others had.[6]

## Columbus in Castile

So he went to Castille, to the court of king Ferdinand and queen Isabella, to tell them of his plan, remonstrating that he lacked only the means to execute it. At first, he got nowhere. The Queen supported him, though, because of a letter of introduction from Alfonso Quinte-ville, the great Camer-leagut or treasurer[7] to Lord

4. In 1484 João II referred Columbus's proposal to a Junta des Mathemáticas, whose principal members were Diogo Ortiz de Vilhegas, later bishop of Viseu, a Jewish physician named Rodrigo, and José Vizinho, a pupil of Abraham Zacuto's.

5. Thevet has confused two visits made by Columbus to La Rábida in 1485 and 1491. During his first visit in 1485, Columbus met Antonio de Marchena, who introduced him to the Duke of Medina Celi. In 1491, Columbus went to La Rábida again and met Juan Perez. This confusion appears to be based on the testimony of Dr. Garcia Fernandez in Palos in 1513. For more details, see Morison, *Admiral*, 1:108–10.

6. The duke of Medina-Sidonia, Don Enrique de Guzmán, was at the time the wealthiest and most powerful aristocrat in Spain. His properties were centered around the port of Sanlúcar, at the mouth of the Guadalquivir. The other important figure in the region, Don Luis de la Cerda, the duke of Medina Celi, also had the means to finance Columbus's enterprise.

7. Alfonso de Quintanilla was *contador mayor* (chief treasurer and accountant) to Ferdinand

Pedro Gonzales de Mendozza, the Archbishop of Toledo, so he did better after a while.

### CONDITIONS AND RESOURCES WHICH FERDINAND, KING OF SPAIN, PROPOSED TO COLUMBUS TO REALIZE HIS UNDERTAKING

After he had attended to the campaign in Granada which was preoccupying him, therefore, the king granted Columbus the right to make his voyage, and assigned to him one tenth of any royal rents or tributes coming from any lands he might discover or acquire. In so much as the king did not have any money for this expedition, Luis his secretary[8] loaned him seventeen thousand ducats, by means of which Columbus outfitted a large ship and two caravels, and hired one hundred twenty men, both soldiers and sailors. He made Martin Alfonso Pinzon the navigator of one caravel, Martin's brothers Francisco Vincente and Aeneas the navigator of the other and, with his brother Bartholomew on board, took the helm and command of the ship himself.[9]

### COLUMBUS'S DEPARTURE FOR THE NEW WORLD

He left Paly on Friday, the third of August, in the year 1492. The difficulties he had getting funding for his voyage paled into insignificance beside those of the trip itself, because of the lack of victuals for his men, who were on the point of mutiny or murder. Even after they had safely reached land, they could not abide him, because of the rigor he had shown toward any who shirked their duty, as the course of this story will make more abundantly clear. Having sailed for several days and finding no land, the soldiers began to grumble, but these were as nothing compared to the threats which led them

and Isabella.

8.   Luis de Santangel, a member of Ferdinand's inner circle, treasurer of the house of Aragon, and a prominent businessman in his own right, had connections with Genoese and Florentine merchants established in Seville and Córdoba who were seeking investment opportunities.

9.   Thevet's "Francisco Vincente" Pinzon is a mistaken transcription of Gómara's Vicente Yáñez Pinzón; see *Historia general*, 1:43. The crew lists given by Morison (*Admiral*, 1:190–91) do not show that Bartholomew was on board the *Santa Maria* with Columbus.

actually to mutiny after having drifted thirty five more days.

### COLUMBUS'S SOLDIERS COMPLAINING

Our poor Genoan was at a loss: all he could think to offer them by way of payment [523v] was a prayer to be a little more patient. But the term for redemption of the prayer was so long that the sweet water began to run out, and they began to cry all the louder that he had to give up and turn back or they would throw him in the sea. They pressed the unhappy captain so hard that he promised to turn back if they did not discover land in three days.

### COLUMBUS WAS THE FIRST TO DISCOVER THE NEW WORLD

The next day, Columbus took in his sails, quite sure that they could not be far from land, because of the freshness of the air and of the little clouds which are seen over land low on the horizon when the sun rises. The following night, the eleventh of November [October], 1492, Rhoderic [Rodrigo], an excellent sailor from Lepe, having climbed to the crow's nest of one of the vessels, shouted "Take heart! I see a fire." Salsede, [Diego de Salcedo] Columbus's servant, quickly reported that his master had already said the same thing. In fact, two hours after midnight the previous night, he had called a Spanish gentlemen named Escobedo, a member of the king's own suite [*valet de chambre du roi*], and told him that he saw a fire, and that in his opinion they were not far from land.[10]

### COLUMBUS'S ENTRY INTO THE NEW WORLD

The first land they saw was Guanabay [Guanahaní], one of the Lucaye islands, situated between Florida and Cuba, where they took summary possession of the New World.[11] From there, they went to

10. Rodrigo de Escobedo was secretary and notary of Columbus's fleet. He drew up official deeds, in the name of the crown, for all lands of which Columbus took possession.

11. Cf. Gómara, *Historia general*, 1:43. Thevet omitted the last part of Gómara's sentence, which attributes the discovery of the New World to Columbus and to Castile. A recent summary of the theories about the site of Columbus's landfall is in Josiah Marvel and Robert

Barucon [Barucoa], a port in Cuba, and took a few Indians. Then they returned to Haiti and anchored in the harbor, which Columbus named [Port] Royal. Then they debarked hurriedly, for the largest ship struck a rock and foundered. The Indians were so frightened, seeing the fire sticks that could strike from so far away, that they left the shore and took refuge in the mountains. So the only one Columbus and his party could capture was a woman, to whom they gave some bread, wine and preserves, along with a shirt and some other clothes. This drew all the other inhabitants of the region who, seeing the courtesy with which the woman was caressed, rushed toward the Spaniards, who exchanged breviaries, glass and bells and other such trinkets for gold, birds, bread and other things. Christopher Columbus and Goacanagari or Guacanari [Guacanagarí], one of the Caciques exchanged many accolades and presents.

### COLUMBUS'S RETURN FROM HIS FIRST TRIP

Our Genoan could not see the hour of his return to Spain, to tell the Catholic king everything he had seen and done. In order to keep his acquisitions secure and with the assent of the chief, he had a castle in wood and mud built and garrisoned it with thirty- eight Spaniards under the orders of captain Roderic d'Arma de Cardove [Cordoba] [524r].[12] As soon as the castle was finished, he took ten Indian men, forty parrots, several tortuses, rabbits and other such things unlike our animals which he put in the ships with all the gold that the natives had given in exchange for their trinkets. In fifty days, with the wind at their backs, they arrived at Paly. Since the King and Queen had heard that there was a way to conquer these countries and draw inestimable treasure from them, given the plenitude of gold which was to be found in the mountains of this country, they sent a much more powerful army back to the country under Columbus's orders.

H. Power, "In Quest of Where America Began: The Case for Grand Turk," *American History Illustrated* 25 (1991):48–69, esp. 55.

12. Morison (*Admiral*, 1:394) says that Columbus left thirty-nine men under the command of Diego de Harana, marshal of the fleet and cousin of Columbus's mistress. Thevet refers, incorrectly, to Diego's father, Rodrigo, following Gómara (*Historia general*, 1:45).

## COLUMBUS'S SECOND TRIP TO THE NEW WORLD

After having confirmed the terms and privileges of his appointment in the city of Barcelona on the twenty-eighth of May, 1493, they sent him back with churchmen, artisans, horses, cows, sheep, goats, pigs and donkeys in order to people the country with them. The expedition left the port of Calis [Cadiz] on the twenty-fifth of September in the year of our Lord 1493, with much more joy than the first crossing. But he was sharply disappointed, for he learned as soon as he arrived at the isle of Haiti, called Espanola, that the thirty-eight that he had left in the fortress under Roderic's [Diego's] orders had been killed by the natives for the vexations, extortions and violence done to them, their goods, and to the honor and virtue of the women. He did not dare punish the Indians at this point, but preferred to save their punishment for another time. Having landed, therefore, he built a village that he named Isabella then, at the mines of Cibao[13] from which gold was being taken, a fortress [St. Thomas] to defend themselves from the violence of the Indians, and left his brother Bartholomew as Governor of the island.[14] Meanwhile he left with three caravels and discovered the southern coast of the isle of Cuba and the island of Jamaica, among others. He returned hence to the isle of Espanola where, having found a good deep water harbor, he named it Saint Nicolas.

## RIOT AT ISABELLA

He had every intention of exterminating the Caribbean Indians, but his sickness prevented him from doing so, and the riot at Isabella, which happened because of the insults, excesses, and indignities which the Spaniards visited upon the natives, setting a bad example for the chiefs and all the natives. In order to regain their friendship, he put to death all the Spaniards who had been responsible for these crimes. This punishment of the Spaniards, and particularly

13.   The central region of Hispaniola.

14.   Thevet is confused here. Diego remained behind as head of a governing council. Columbus left Bartholomew as *adelantado* at Isabella when he returned to Spain after his second expedition.

of Gaspar Freiz from Aragon,[15] whom Columbus had hanged, stung the other Spaniards so sharply that, the minute he was cured of his malady, there was nothing for it but for him to set sail for Spain to defend himself against the accusations brought against him by those who defended the garrisons. In fact, the king had already sent his Chamberlain Juan Aguado[16] to America to send Columbus back to Spain as a prisoner. He arrived at Court at Medina del Campo[17] and, after giving [524v] the king and the queen their presents, started immediately to defend his punishment of the Spaniards. He did such a good job of whitewashing that the king declared him absolved of all the crimes with which he had been slandered, and furnished him with eightships to go search for other countries.

### COLUMBUS'S THIRD VOYAGE

Columbus sent two ships ahead with victuals and ammunition, and left with the other six from Saint Luke of Barrameda on the twenty-eighth of May in the year 1497,[18] and set sail for Madeira, one of the seven Portuguese islands which they call the Azores. He sent three ships thence straight to Espanola with three hundred men. He sailed with the three others down to Cape Verde and, from there, set sail for the Indies along the equator. Having arrived and entered the Gulf of Paria,[19] he anchored near the island of Cubagua, which he named Pearl Island.

15.   Gómara is the only source we have found that mentions "Gaspar Férriz, aragonés" (*Historia general*, 1:56).

16.   Juan de Aguado, a former member of the queen's household, accompanied Columbus on his second voyage and later returned to Spain with Antonio de Torres. He investigated Columbus's conduct and issued a report on his activities as viceroy and governor.

17.   Columbus returned to Burgos, not Medina del Campo. Thevet probably copied this mistake from Gómara (*Historia general*, 1:57).

18.   Columbus departed from Sanlúcar de Barrameda, the port of Seville at the mouth of the Guadalquivir in 1498, not 1497. Thevet has again duplicated an error by Gómara (ibid., 1:58), although the latter did not place Madeira in the Azores. Most sources give May 30, rather than May 28, as the date of departure.

19.   The Gulf of Paria opens in front of the mouth of the Orinoco River on the coast of Venezuela.

## Roldan Ximenes

Columbus, having made several sorties against the local inhabitants and discovered several new islands, became the object of envy on the part of the Spaniards. He wrote to Roldan Ximenes,[20] the grand Podesta or judge, ordering him to recognize Columbus's authority, but Ximenes took no account of the order. He conspired with seventy men to mutiny, and left Columbus for Siraguo [Xaragua]. He wrote many complaints against Columbus and his brothers to the king, who was quite displeased that things were going so badly in the Indies, and sent Sir Francisco de Bovaldello [Francisco de Bobadilla] to be their Governor.

## The Columbuses Sent to Spain as Prisoners

The latter arrived at Espanola with a fleet of four caravels in the year 1499[21] and, having made an investigation in the city of Santo Domingo, sent Christopher Columbus and his brothers Bartholomew and Diego to Spain as prisoners in leg irons.[22]

## Columbus's fourth voyage

When the king heard them, he found so little merit in the calumnious accusations against them that, knowing Columbus's loyalty, Ferdinand sent Columbus back with four caravels to look for new lands three years later, on the ninth of May in the year 1502. When he came back to the island of Espanola, close to the Ocana [Ozama] river, Nicolas d'Ouanda,[23] govenor of the Island, refused to allow him to enter the city of Santo Domingo. Columbus was very angry at being refused entry, since it was he who had built the city. He

20.   Francisco Roldán served as *alcalde mayor* of the island of Isabella.

21.   Gómara, in his account of this voyage, mistakenly placed it in 1499 rather than in 1500. *Historia general*, 1:61. Thevet apparently copied this mistake.

22.   Columbus was sent home in chains along with Diego, but Bartholomew appears to have been on another ship. Morison, *Admiral*, 2:303. Gómara had both brothers being sent back with Columbus. *Historia general*, 1:61.

23.   Nicholas de Ovando, knight commander of Lares and governor of Hispaniola, had arrived in Santo Domingo in April.

set sail toward the West, and discovered the isle of Guanaxo [Gua-nacca], close to a part of the continent that the natural inhabitants of the country call Higuera, and the Spaniards, the Cape of Honduras. Then he left there, and drifting along the coast toward the West, found the country of Veraguil [Veragua] and set foot in the islands of Zorobaro [Isla Colón], which are not too far from the continent and which, according to the inhabitants of the region [525r] as well as those of Veragua, was rich in gold. He pressed on upon hearing this report, still keeping close to the coast until he reached the Gulf of Uraba, where he landed and discovered the Southern Sea.[24] He returned thence to Cuba, then to Jamaica, where he lost two ships. He continued his search for new lands with the two remaining ships, but not without suffering grievous dangers and discomforts: his men fell sick, and even the Spaniards fought against him. The Indians took full advantage of his discomfiture, seeing that Francisco de Po-raz [Porras], captain of one caravel, and Diego, Columbus's brother, had taken a few barques to sail for Espanola.[25] Columbus found himself in such tight straits that he ran short of victuals, and could not obtain any by exchange, entreaties, love, nor force.

### Columbus's Trick To Obtain Victuals

Necessity being the mother of invention, Columbus sent word to some inhabitants of a nearby village that, if they did not give him foodstuffs, God would shortly send such a punishment from the heavens that they would all die in agony. As a sign of the vengeance to come, he told them that they would see the moon all red with blood if they looked at it. When they saw the moon bloodied (by the eclipse) as the Admiral had predicted, they gave him all the food he needed for all the time he stayed on this island, begging him all the while to forgive them and not to be angry with them.

---

24. Columbus, of course, did not discover the Pacific Ocean, which Thevet and many of his contemporaries called the South or Southern Sea. He correctly identifies Balboa as the discoverer of the Pacific in the chapter on Magellan.

25. This information is found in Benzoni, *History of the New World*, ed. and trans. Smyth, 42–43, and Gómara, *Historia general*, 1:63, but the brothers Francisco and Diego de Porras (rather than Columbus's brother Diego) sailed for Española.

## DEATH OF COLUMBUS

After all his travails, the expert navigator was seized by a sickness at Vaglidolit [Valladolid] which killed him on the eighth [twentieth] of May in the year 1506. In his will, he ordered that his body be born to Seville, to the monastery of Certosa.[26] The following epitaph was composed in his honor:[27]

> With someone else's ships and your own intellect,
> > You discovered a new world and new people,
> > Magnanimous Columbus, where other winds
> > Gave your sails the signal to run.
>
> Those rough people, an affront to Heaven,
> > Who worshipped, instead of gods, running springs,
> > Laden trees, or beautiful and bright flowers,
> > You made them revere the Lord of the Sacred Kingdom.
>
> Not satisfied with this, you taught them
> > Human laws, holy matrimony,
> [525v] And you built cities girt with walls.
>
> And yet, since you have benefitted her so much,
> > Does India call you Father: Jove gives you, among the
> > > others, glory.

## CHILDREN OF CHRISTOPHER COLUMBUS

He left two sons, Diego, who was married to Mary of Toledo, daughter of Ferdinand, grand commander of Leon, and Ferdinand, who did not marry.

---

26. More detailed information is in Morison, "Appendix of the Remains of Columbus," in *Admiral*, 2:423–26. The Dominican historian Carlos Dobal has suggested that half of Columbus's remains may be found in Valladolid or in the monastery of La Cartuja de Santa María de las Cuevas; he thinks that the other half of Columbus's remains—the right side and both feet—is in the Dominican Republic. See *Quincentennial of the Discovery of America: Encounter of Two Worlds*, Newsletter of the Organization of American States, no. 28 (Aug. 1991): 15.

27. This epitaph, by Giovanni Vitali, is found in Giovio's *Gli elogi vite brevemente*, f.177.

## Ferdinand's Rich Library

He had a library of more than twelve thousand volumes which is at present at the monastery of Saint Dominic of Seville. The library was worthy of the son of such a father.

## The Spaniards Would Like to Steal from Columbus the Honor of Having Discovered the West Indies

The Spaniards tried to steal the honor of having discovered the West Indies from Columbus and give it to the Andalusian captain, a merchant who had been plying his trade in [the] Canary [Islands] and Madeira when he undertook his long and perilous journey. He died in Columbus's house, where the log books from the caravel remained, with indications of the latitude of the newly discovered lands, which is how Columbus knew the location of the Indies.[28] The fact that he was a good humanist and knowledgeable cosmographer gave him the idea of looking for the Antipodes and rich Cipango [Japan], about which a Venetian named Marco Polo had written. Also, since he read Plato's Timaeus and Crito, where he speaks of a great island called Atlantis, and of a land inundated by a deluge which was greater than Asia and Africa put together. In addition, having read that Aristotle, writing to Theophrastus, says in his The Wonders of the World that some Carthaginian merchants, sailing past the straits of Gibraltar to the South and East, had discovered after sailing a long time a great island, uninhabited but well provided with everything necessary for life, and blessed with large navigable rivers.[29]

28. This story about the so-called "Andalusian Captain" or "Unknown Pilot" began to circulate shortly after Columbus's discovery of 1492. Oviedo first published it in 1535, and other Spanish authorities repeated it throughout the sixteenth century. For translations of relevant documents and histories, see Thacher, *Christopher Columbus*, 1:325–44, 3:470–72.

29. Thevet may be referring to *Concerning the Wonders of Nature*, a compilation of pseudo-Aristotelian propositions compiled by a Fray Teófilo de Ferraris. The identity of the island founded by Carthaginian merchants was a matter of controversy even in Ferdinand Columbus's biography of his father. See *The Life and Times of the Admiral*, ed. Keen, 29–34.

## COLUMBUS'S CLEVER TRICK TO SILENCE HIS DETRACTORS

All I shall say in response to such envious accusations is what Columbus himself said in response to a group of Spanish nobles talking one feast day about the discovery of the Indies. The discussion grew so heated that Columbus asked that an egg be brought to him and said to all of them, that there was no one in the party who could keep the egg up without touching it. After each had tried, he took the egg and rapped one end on the table so that, having slightly broken it, he was able to keep it upright.[30]

30. This popular story apparently originated with Benzoni, *History of the New World*, ed. Smyth, 17.

'HEVREVX fuccés du voyage de Chriſto-
phle Colomb, qui a eſté propoſé cy deſſus,
reſueilla pluſieurs Princes à dreſſer & equip-
per nauires, pour enuoier auſſi bien que le
Roy de Caſtille à l'emploicte & recouure-
ment des pays, qui eſtans incogneus, & ſans
maiſtres (au moins receus & approuués) ſem
bloient par droiċt de conqueſte, appartenir
au premier qui pourroit les impieter. Entre autres le preſent diſcours
repreſéter a l'expeditiō, que fit le Roy de Portugal pour deſcouurir

*Expedition
du Roy de
Portugal au
monde nou-
ueau.*

# Amerigo Vespucci

The success of Christopher Columbus's expedition, of which we spoke above, inspired several rulers to build and outfit ships to send, like those sent by the King of Castille [Ferdinand of Aragon], to seize and exploit unknown lands without rulers (or at least without commonly recognized and approved ones) which seemed to belong by right of conquest to the first to trod on them. Among other things the present discourse will represent the expedition which the King of Portugal undertook to discover [526v] the new world. We can be quite sure that he bit his nails to the quick when he noticed that the person who had offered to recover these lands for him had acquired a great many for the King of Castille, and that the latter's kingdom overflowed with gold, pearls, and other precious commodities.

## Expedition to the New World By the King of Portugal

For this reason, he outfitted three ships and sent them, under the command of this Florentine, to the lands that had so enriched Ferdinand and his kingdom. I shall not tarry over the dangers and perils, the rocks upon which the storms of their voyage threw them, as Vespucci himself tells it.[1] They were on the point of foundering

---

1. Here Thevet is probably referring to *Mundus novus. Albericus Vesputius Laurentio petri de medicis Salutem plurimum dicit*, the first printed document about Brazil. This letter, ostensibly written by Vespucci himself to Lorenzo di Pier Francesco de Medici, contributed more than anything else to the former's reputation and went through many editions in Latin, Italian, French, German, Flemish, and Czech in the first half of the sixteenth century. It is impossible to determine which edition(s) Thevet knew: details about the various editions are in Roberto Levillier, "Mundus novus. La carta de Vespuccio que revolucionó geografiá (édicion crítica)," *Boletín del Instituto de Historia Argentina "Doctor Emilio Ravignani,"* ser. 2, 1 (1956):5–118, esp. 12–25.

several times, not only because of the severity of the storms but also because of the small size of the crew, compared to the normal size for such an undertaking.

## VESPUCCI THE GUIDE, LEADER, AND BOSS ON THE SHIP

He had to navigate, command, and explore on his own, even though there were expert sailors in the company, because they had no idea where they were, since they were unacquainted with Cosmographie [geography]. This caused him to be all the more admired by all, particularly crew members who being ignorant of this science, held this Florentine navigator in very high repute.[2]

## VESPUCCI'S EXPLOIT UPON DISCOVERING NEW LANDS

On the 14th of May in the year 1501, he left Olisippa [Lisbon] with these three ships, came round Cape Verde, and sailed continuously for twenty months [days],[3] and discovered the Island of Borriquen [Puerto Rico] and the Florida Peninsula. Having penetrated to the Islands of St. Jean[4] and Cuba, he anchored at the Isthmus which we commonly call *Nombre de Dios*, some ten and a half degrees of latitude from the Equator. Having sailed along the coast to the province of the Caribes,[5] where he stayed for two months waiting for favorable winds, and skirting the Island of Trinidad, he went off again to landfall in the gulf which lies between two great rivers, the Aureillane [Orellana] and the Marignan [Marañon], which we commonly call the river of the Amazons, next to the Promontory of

2.    Thevet has taken this information from *Mundus novus*. We have used the edition by Levillier, *Américo Vespucio*, 301.

3.    Although great controversy exists about almost all aspects of Vespucci's voyages, the reality of the 1501–2 expedition has never been contested. For discussions of relevant issues and documents see Borba de Moraes, *Bibliographia Brasiliana*, 2:345–50, and Morison, *The European Discovery of America*, 304–12. Thevet copied this error about "twenty months" from *Mundus novus*, ed. Levillier, 173 n.1.

4.    This may also be a reference to Puerto Rico, which Columbus named San Juan Bautista. Gómara refers to it both as St. Joan and St. Juan. *Historia general*, 1:65, 94.

5.    The Carib Indians inhabited the Lesser Antilles and parts of the neighboring South American coast. Their name, whose Arawakian equivalent is the provenance of the word *Cannibal*, was given to the Caribbean Sea.

Cannibals [Cabo Santo Agostinho].[6] Reversing his sails, he put out straight for Ethiopia. This is why many think that he was the first to discover the greatest part of America. This is the reason he is praised by many, among others by a Tuscan who wrote these verses:[7]

> Let who will wish that he had been born in an ancient time,
> And let him believe the previous centuries were better than
> more recent ones.
> It gratifies me that I saw the light in recent years:
> In my opinion the old times are inferior to the recent ones.
> The ancient age had been neither more favorable to discoveries,
> Nor did the minds possess greater sharpness than today.
> Add the fact that this age benefits from advantages which [527r]
> provided though they were by the diligence of the old times,
> were nonetheless enriched by the diligence of recent times.
> Not to mention, however, the rest of the beneficial advantages
> of our century,
> the more recent time makes better use of old time advantages.
> Shall I fail to mention how many benefits the new world has
> supplied with a daring ship, having left behind the
> Straits of Gibraltar?
> And shall I omit the fact that the pepper and treasures of
> the Orient come to the West frequently by an easy route?
> And shall I omit you, Americus, if the ancient Jason is compared
> to you it will be said that he sailed across the watery passages
> with a fearful ship?
> Tell me which of the kings names after himself a greater part
> of the world or adorns it with his claims to glory?
> In this you are best, Americus, you were born a private citizen
> on the river Arno: and after your claim to glory is
> America named, and deservedly so: it was discovered and
> conquered by your war exploits.
> With a region practically as big as half of the immense earth,
> thus you make your own time more important than the ancient
> one by as much as the half is usually lesser than the whole.

6. See Thevet's chapter on Nacol-absou, "King of the Promontory of the Cannibals."

7. This epitaph was taken from Giovanni Matteo Toscano, *Peplus Italiae* (Paris, 1578), bk. 1, no. 46:28–29.

### Vespucci did not discover America

According to them, then, this fourth part of the world owes its name to the Florentine Americus. I cannot agree, however, with those who would inadvisedly credit him with the discovery of these countries, for they forget that two years before

### Vincente Pinzon

Captain Vincente Pinzon, an expert navigator, a courageous man and more fortunate sailor, had sailed more than eight hundred leagues further South, but he had not the gift to commit his exploits as a navigator to writing.

### Vespucci, because he wrote of the success of his trip, is credited with being the first to discover the new lands

Vespucci has made off with the prize for having let the world know about America, because he described his voyage, though he did so in a heavy and crude style.[8] By so doing, he not only robbed Pinzon of the credit he earned, but also the Genoan Columbus, who has partisans who will not allow the Florentine to bedeck himself with Columbine plumage, which could only be inappropriate and ill-fitting to him.[9] If there were disagreement between the authors over the discovery of America, I find even more over the description of its figure and form.

### The error of Ortelius and other geographers

I remember having mentioned in my Cosmographie the error of some other Geographers who, in order to separate America from Asia, have fabricated a strait [527v] in the most inappropriate way

8.   Thevet may be referring to *Lettera di Amerigo Vespucci delle isole novamente trovate in quattro suoi viaggi,* ed. Levillier, in which the author apologized for his barbarous style and lack of learning (308).

9.   See Justin Winsor, "Critical and Bibliographical Notes on Vespuccius and the Naming of America," in *Narrative and Critical History,* ed. Winsor, 2 (1886):153–79, for an excellent survey on contemporary opinion about whether Columbus or Vespucci discovered America.

imaginable.[10] It is therefore all the more astonishing that Abraham Ortelius found himself unable to avoid falling into this mistake in his first chart of the Theater of the Universe,[11] since I had written amply enough on the matter to relieve him of any doubt that might remain. Perhaps this worthy personage preferred the opinions of Gemma Frisius, Giacomo Castaldi from the Piedmont, Giovanni Baptista Guicciardin,[12] together with several other serious and worthy personages to the simple truth on the matter, which I can assure all of having discovered, having had the good fortune of seeing with my own eyes what they learned solely from the reports of others. Even though I have no desire to tarnish in any way the authority due to such exceptional minds, nonetheless I daresay (without flattering myself with too high an opinion of myself) that the testimony which I was able to offer on this score is worth more than the hearsay of others, as our French Homer put it,[13]

The eye, as witness, is more trustworthy than the ear.

### THE VOYAGES OF MARTIN FORBISHER, ENGLISHMAN

The English Ambassador took much more careful account of my opinions, when he was charged with learning from me the secrets necessary for the English Captain Martin Forbisher's exploration of the West and Northwest, toward the North Pole, in the year 1567.[14]

10.   *Cosmographie universelle*, 2:f.911r, 1025r.

11.   Thevet is referring to Ortelius, *Theatrum orbis terrarum*, 1st ed. (Antwerp, 1570), the most popular atlas of engraved maps of its time.

12.   Gemma Frisius, Mercator's teacher and a celebrated cartographer in his own right, showed a northern strait called *fretum arcticum sive trium fratrum* (after the Corte-Real brothers) on his 1537 map. The Piedmontese cartographer Giacomo Gastaldi made numerous maps between 1544 and 1570, and in 1562 published a pamphlet first naming the "Strait of Anian." Giovanni Baptista Guiccardini made a world map in the form of a double-headed eagle (Antwerp, 1549). For Gastaldi's pamphlet, see R. A. Skelton, *Explorer's Maps* (London, 1958), 117, n.5.

13.   We do not know to whom Thevet is referring here.

14.   We have not found these details about Thevet's relations with an English ambassador elsewhere. Later (ca. 1586), in "Grand insulaire" (f.403v), he repeated his complaint about Frobisher, "who for five years has been beating his brains out to pass from the [Atlantic] Sea to that of the South through this northern detour."

Against the advice of many, I told him of the sights and secrets of those areas. Had they taken the trouble to pursue what I said, they would not have so mistakenly looked for their Northern passage, which these noble Geographers also contrived to find hidden in the Antarctic. They led this English Captain and several others into trying many voyages with small chance of success, putting their lives and the wealth backing their expeditions at a risk which would have been better placed elsewhere. I have been forced into this digression by the fact that I see many who consider themselves well-endowed with intelligence insisting on the pleasure of locking themselves into this supposed strait. It would, however, appear that I entered into this digression in order to accumulate praise for myself. Better that I teach those who can barely read the mistake they make by saying that the King of Spain possesses most of America. In addition to the lands subject to the Kings of France and Portugal, there remain more than five hundred parts which Spain does not rule.

## FERNAND MAGELLAN, PORTVGAIS.

### Chapitre 102.

E v x, qui ont voulu mettre en contrepois le deuoir d'obeiſſance & fidelité, que doit le ſubiect à ſon ſuperieur, auec les reigles, qui doiuent eſtre obſeruées par ceux, qui plus haut eſleués que les autres, ont moyen, pouuoir & authorité de commander, ont treſ-à-propos remarqué qu'il y a vn meſmes point, alentour duquel, comme du centre, tous les cercles ſelõ leur proportiõnée circõferẽce doiuẽt eſtre tournés. Et à ceſte occaſiõ ont cõpaſſé, & limité, au mieux qu'ils ont peu, par leur

# FERDINAND MAGELLAN, PORTUGUESE

Those who have sought to trade off the duty of obedience and fidelity, which the subject owes to his superior, against the rules which the nobly born—those who have the means and the authority to command—ought to observe, have quite rightly remarked that there is a point, like a center, around which all circles should be turned, according to their proportional circumferences. They have encompassed and limited in this way, to the best of their ability, [528v] everything they thought to be required of all parties, so that they might acquit themselves of their obligations. But they could not round the contours of this center so successfully that no obligation escaped to deform their circular forms.[1]

## THE TWO GREAT PRINCIPLES OF CIVIL GOVERNMENT

I could well use several points here which can be noted in political administration, were it not my fear of prolixity, in which I would be quite wrong to fall, since the foundation of civil police is now represented for us in the two great principles: to wit, the punishment of evildoers and criminals, and the reward of those who deserve to have their virtues recognized. I shall leave the discourse on punishments to one side, since the present subject does not call for it, and shall remark in the example of this Portuguese the wise consideration which must be given in compensation for those who labor

---

1. Thevet's reference here to "circular forms" is unclear, but he may be referring to Jeronymo Osorio's *De nobilitate civile et christiana* (Lisbon, 1542; English tr. William Blandie, *A Discourse of Civill and Christian Nobilitie* [London, 1576]).

for the commonwealth. This gentleman had been Captain of several Portuguese ships of war in the conflicts of the Indies as well as those against the Moors in Barbary.

## THE KING OF PORTUGAL REFUSES AN INCREASE IN MAGELLAN'S SALARY OF SIX DUCATS PER YEAR

Upon his return, he asked the king to augment his wages by half a ducat per month, maintaining that the great and dangerous travails which he had undergone during his long service to the crown deserved no less an increase. The king denied his request, fearing to open the way to ambitious and importune demands. To say that it was the size of the amount itself that caused the king to refuse would be to fool oneself on purpose, since six ducats a year would have been a bargain, at bottom. But this good king considered that a court is most often furnished with several leaches, so that, had he accorded Magellan his request, he was opening the way for others to ask for more.[2] I am well aware that I shall now be belabored with many Histories of princes who showered their special favorites with liberal awards, without being forced to grant the same favors to all those who had made similar requests. But if the outcome was unhappy (as it was), why not excuse this King of Portugal, who preferred to refuse six ducats a year to Magellan to depleting his treasury by immense gifts or sowing jealousy between Magellan and his other captains, to whom he did not wish to give raises?

## MAGELLAN'S REVOLT AGAINST THE KING OF PORTUGAL

Nonetheless, Magellan, showing scant regard for such considerations, conceived such a resentment in his mind that, forgetting all faith, piety and religion, he did not rest until (at least as far as he was able) he had betrayed the king who had brought him up and his native country and, putting his life at great risk, had put the state in

---

2. The principal source of information about Magellan's expedition, Antonio Pigafetta, corroborated these details in a section of his account that remained unpublished in the sixteenth century. See *Magellan's Voyage*, ed. and trans. Skelton, 1:116.

great [529r] danger.[3] In order to have his vengeance, he seized the opportunity offered him by a Portuguese friend and relation, named Francisco Serran [Serrão], Royal Governor of Tarenate [Ternate], who had often begged him to go to that country.[4]

### MAGELLAN'S OVERTURE TO THE KING OF SPAIN, TO RECOVER THE MOLUQUES [SPICE] ISLANDS

He decided to recover the Moluques by another way than by the East, with the support of King Charles, to whom he had access through Francisco Ximenes, Cardinal and governor of the entire kingdom.[5] He gave the King to understand that the Moluques Islands, situated beyond the golden Chersonese,[6] belonged rightfully to the King of Spain, and that Emanuel, King of Portugal, was usurping them under false pretenses, against the agreement between the Castilians and the Portuguese.[7] The better to impress this opinion upon Charles's mind, he brought Roderick Falier with him, who claimed to be a great cosmographer, and an even greater astrologer.[8] He showed the King by evident demonstrations the truth of his man Magellan's assertions, along with the great profit that would accrue from such a voyage so that, by this route, spices and other merchandise could be brought from the East at lesser cost and in greater security than the Portuguese were able to do, because of the great detour they

3.   Here Thevet follows *Histoire de Portugal*, ed. and trans. Goulart, almost verbatim. The "great danger" is the threat of war between Spain and Portugal.

4.   After being shipwrecked at Banda, Francisco Serrão entered the service of the sultan of Ternate. His correspondence with Magellan exerted a strong influence on the latter's plans for an expedition to find the southern strait. See ibid., 305 and Pigafetta's account, *Magellan's Voyage*, ed. and trans. Skelton, 1:116. Magellan's relationship to Serrão is unknown.

5.   After Ferdinand the Catholic's death in 1516, Cardinal Ximénes successfully managed Charles I's accession to the throne.

6.   Ramusio, who published part of Pigafetta's relation in *Primo volume*, defined the term as the old name for Malacca; we have used the Venice 1606 edition, f.347r.

7.   The treaty of Tordesillas (1494) divided the newly discovered lands between Spain and Portugal at a line 370 degrees west of the Cape Verde Islands.

8.   Roderick Falier, or Ruy Faleiro, a Portuguese cosmographer, also renounced his nationality and accompanied Magellan to Spain to offer his services to Charles I. Before he went insane, he played an important role in securing support for Magellan's enterprise. See Gómara, *Historia general*, 1:214; *Histoire de Portugal*, ed. and trans. Goulart, 430.

were forced to make around the Cape of Good Hope. I shall not try here to prove either of these Kings correct. Even if the King of Spain had every right to this territory, Magellan's cause would not have been stronger, since his reason for undertaking to recover the Moluques Islands was not to aggrandize the state of Castille, but rather to use the power and authority of King Charles in order to avenge the wrong by which he felt himself aggrieved.

### MAGELLAN GENERAL OF THE ARMY OF THE KING OF SPAIN, FOR THE DISCOVERY OF THE MOLUQUES [SPICE] ISLANDS

To return, then, to Magellan, the hour was so propitious for his undertaking that Charles, without being offended by the revolt of this Portuguese man, made him General of a fleet of five ships which he outfitted at his own expense, with full powers of life and death over the Captains, soldiers, navigators, and sailors. He set sail from the port of Seville, and from the port of San Lucar de Barrameda, the tenth day of August, 1519, taking with him 237 men, soldiers as well as sailors. The flagship was named Trinity, the others Victory, Saint Anthony, Conception, and Saint James. I do not wish to set forth each detail of their discovery, I shall restrict myself to recounting a few singular events which happened on their trip. Among others, the frights, dangers, and scrapes of all sorts in which he and his company found themselves several times. He put his men through such travails that several of them, among the least prudent, angry at being hungry, even starving, not only complained about him as well, [529v] but also dared to conspire against his life, which so angered him that, to quiet their sedition, as soon as they entered Port, leaving Saint Julian's,

### EXECUTION OF MUTINEERS AND CONSPIRATORS AGAINST MAGELLAN

[he] had the treasurer Luis de Mendozza drawn, beheaded Gaspard de Casade [Casado], and put Juan de Cartagena ashore, with a priest, to cause them to die of hunger there and to place them at the mercy of their enemies, giving them a small sack of biscuit and only their

swords for weapons.[9] By these means, he softened the others considerably.

## STRAIT OF MAGELLAN

As soon as they left this harbor, they headed around thirty leagues further South, to fifty- two degrees from the South Pole, and found, finally, in the year 1520 the important strait which (if we were to believe Osorius) would only be twenty leagues long and (according to the others) is 110 leagues long, and approximately two leagues wide. It is at a latitude of fifty-two degrees thirty minutes and longitude of three hundred three degrees. It was he who discovered it first at midnight, while the Captains of the other ships thought it was some gulf with no exit.[10] But he knew there was a well-hidden strait, which he had seen marked on a naval map made by a great navigator, named Martin de Boëme, in the library of the King of Portugal.[11] And for this reason the strait was called the Strait of Magellan. Having cleared the strait the 28th of November of this year, he turned the prows of his ships to the right, and took the route which almost seemed to go behind the sun to regain the Equator: they entered the Peaceful [Pacific] Sea discovered by Vast Numez de Valboa [Balboa],[12] where they bobbed for three months and twenty days before seeing land. During this time, they suffered greatly from lack of victuals and other afflictions, which caused them several maladies, such as swelling of the jaws and gastro-intestinal disorders caused by the bad food and spoiled drink that they took. Nineteen died, and twenty-five or thirty

9. In *Life of Ferdinand Magellan*, Guillemard identified the priest as Pero Sanchez de Reina (171). Details of the mutiny at Port St. Julien are given in Skelton's edition of Pigafetta's account (1:154, n.2).

10. Except for the reference to 303 degrees of latitude, this geography follows Ramusio (*Primo volume*, f.354v). Osorio's claim that the strait was only twenty leagues wide is in *Histoire de Portugal*, ed. and trans. Goulart, 433. Thevet's assertion that Magellan himself first saw the strait appears to be original.

11. See Franz von Wieser, *Magalhães-Strasse und Austral-Continent auf den Globen des Johannes Schöner* (Innsbruck, 1881); Guillemard, *Life of Magellan*, 188–98; and E. G. Ravenstein, *Martin Behaim, His Life and His Globe* (London, 1908), 34–38.

12. For the argument that Antonio de Abreu discovered the Pacific Ocean in 1511, nearly two years before Balboa sighted it, see Charles E. Nowell, "The Discovery of the Pacific: A Suggested Change of Approach," *Pacific Historical Review* 16 (1947):1–10, esp. 6–7.

fell sick, after having traveled four thousand leagues in this Peaceful Sea.

## ARCHIPELAGO OF SAINT LAZARUS [THE PHILIPPINES]

Having passed the Equator, they encountered many islands, which they named the Archipelago of Saint Lazarus. From island to island, the Spaniards finally reached the isle of Zebut [Cebu], where the King Hamabar received them courteously.

## DEATH OF MAGELLAN

At Matan [Mactan], they had to fight, and there the valiant Captain Magellan was killed by an arrow, which a Matanese shot in his face, the 26th of April 1521, to the great loss of Christianity: for after his death, Hamabar, who had been baptized, revolted and killed Serran, who had been one of Magellan's lieutenants, with thirty Spaniards.[13]

13. *Histoire de Portugal,* ed. and trans. Goulart, 505–6, but for a different account see *Magellan's Voyage,* ed. and trans. Skelton, 1:168, n.32.

# II

# Native Americans

## ATABALIPA, ROY DV PERV.

### Chapitre. 141.

 E s hommes plus nobles, riches & püiſſans de la terre Peruſienne furent les Iugas, peuples felons, belliqueux & ſubtils au poſſible, iſſus d'vn peuple Tiguicata, prenant le nom d'vne ville, ſituée auprés d'vn lac, en la Prouince de Colao, à quelques dix lieües de Cuſco, ainſy nommée, pour l'abondance du plomb & autres métaux, qui ſ'y trouuent, *Parés d'A-* *tabalipa.*
que les habitans appellent *Tichior.* Le premier Roy ſappelloit *Zapalo*
de l'eſtoc duquel vint *Topaopangui* & *Guya nacapa* pere grãd d'Atabalipa

Q Q Q Q q

# Atabalipa,
# King of Peru

The richest, most powerful and noble men of Peru were the Iugas [Incas], as warlike, tricky, and villainous a people as can be imagined, descended from a Tiguicata race and taking the name of a city situated on a lake (which the inhabitants call *Tichior* [Titicaca]) in the province of Colao, some ten leagues distant from Cusco and named for the abundance of lead and other metals found there.

## Parents of Atabalipa [Atahuallpa]

The first king was called *Zapalo*: from his stock came *Topaopangui & Guyanacapa*,[1] grandfather of Atabalipa [641v] who took pride in coming from those parts: the fact is that he had come from the race of Cannibals around the Maragnon river,[2] as he showed clearly enough by the challenges and contempt in which he held Christians, when they set foot in his lands. Still, the people of the region are courteous and peaceful, with sufficient *savoir-faire*, though they do not concern themselves overmuch with the honors and glories of this world, any more than the inhabitants of Cusco, Popaian [Popayán], and the nearby province do.[3]

1.  Thevet here refers to Topa Inca Yupanki (1471–93) and Huayna Capac (1493–1525), predecessors of Atahuallpa. Upon his death, Huayna Capac divided his empire between his sons Huascar and Atahuallpa. Thevet refers to the war between the two heirs below.

2.  The association of the Maráñon River with cannibals is common in the sources. For example, see Belleforest, *Cosmographie universelle*, 2:cols. 2062–74, "Du grand flevve de Maragnon, et des peuples dit Caribes, ou canibales, & leurs façons de vivre."

3.  Thevet appears to have taken the information presented in these sections from Gómara's *Historia general*, 2:chap. 119, "Linaje de Atabaliba."

### ATALBALIPA'S BROTHER ATOCO

Now Atabalipa, king of Cusco, had a brother, named Atoco, who was Iuga [Inca], i.e. king of *Guiascart*.[4] This Atoco was well received and honored by the people when he arrived, in spite of his cruelty. Atabalipa, jealous of the fortune of his brother, put him to death and, having seized his places, chose the city of Cusco for the Capital of the entire kingdom of Peru, since it was the former domicile and resting place of the Iugas and Kings, in the same way that Rome had been for the Emperors, Constantinople for the Turks, Tauris [Tabriz] for Sophy, Catay for the grand Cham of Tartary, and long ago Cairo for the Sultan of Egypt. All the more since Cusco is the most beautiful site of all Peru, and in the middle of the provinces formerly governed by the Iugas.

### ATABALIPA ENLARGES HIS KINGDOM

After the death of Atabalipa's forebears, he enlarged his kingdom to the Pacific as well as the Atlantic, rendering the peoples his tributaries.[5] But, as ill chance and Fortune falls as often on the great as on the small, it happened in my own day that the Spaniards, covetous of earthly riches, voyaged under the command of a great warrior, named Francisco Pizarro, to this land, called Nombre de Dios. Having lived some time there, and having fortified themselves, little by little they attracted the half of these barbarous people who were aware of king Atabalipa's treasure and riches.

### PIZARRO'S COURTESIES TOWARD ATABALIPA

In order to attract his friendship, Pizarro sent him several gifts and presents, giving him to understand that they had been sent by the Christian Emperor, his master, and that he was eager for friendship,

---

4.    Thevet apparently has confused Huascar (Gómara's Guaxcar) with Atoco, who commanded the former's forces at the battle of Ambato. Gómara does not mention Atoco, but his activities are described in other sources; see, for example, *The Incas of Pedro de Cieza de Léon*, trans. H. de Onis, ed. V. W. von Hagen (Norman, 1959), 81, 83–85.

5.    Topa Inca Yupanki and Huayna Capac, rather than Atahuallpa, were responsible for expanding the Incan Empire.

and to talk without fear with his majesty, and that were he to come visit, he should not be offended to see them mounted on great beasts, quite tame, which they had brought from their own country to carry them. Particularly as they had heard of the bad roads, rivers, quicksand, and other inconveniences of his country, in which they could not travel without great danger to their person. The barbarian, hearing these speeches, burst into laughter at the expense of the Spaniards, saying that these bearded men (by which he meant the Spaniards, since they all wore beards), if they undertook to come any further than they had already done, by the sun and Idol which he worshipped, he would have them all cut to pieces.

### Pizarro's trick to surprise Atabalipa

Pizarro refused to be rattled by these threats against him and his [642r] men, but acted as a very valiant warrior: aware that the enemy army had not yet been assembled, that he had only summoned his troops from the provinces of Cusco, Quito, Calicuciua, Caxamalca, Tumbez Pune, Nicaraga a week ago, and that he could hardly gather an army in so few days, Pizarro immediately sent a new present, two well-outfitted horses, to distract the barbarian king a while longer. Approaching little by little, he asked that, before leaving his country, he be allowed to come salute him and see the magnificence and glory of his Court, in order to be able to tell the Emperor about it, who would be most happy to hear of the grandeur and magnificence of such a powerful Lord as Atabalipa was. In order better to ensnare the latter, he made his ears ring with the majesty and excellence of the Emperor, to the point that Christians counted it a great honor to be able to do him obeisance, tempting him thus to try to enter into an alliance with him, so that two such great princes might hold in check any who might harbor ambitions against either of their states, since this is the true means to assure principalities and kingdoms, particularly since it is usually true that force cannot put bodies asunder when they are stiff and robust. But this was not really what Pizarro was looking at in any event, his aim was solely to place his feet on any part of Atabalipa's land, sure in the knowledge that he would shortly be putting it on the latter's throat, as in fact he did thereafter, as the continuation of the present discourse will reveal more clearly.

## THE SPANIARDS SEIZE THE PERUVIANS

This masterful Spaniard soft-soaped [*ioüa si bien du plat de la langue*] and fooled him with so many tricks that he came with all his cavalry and infantry to reconnoiter the enemy forces with his officers near the city of *Cassiamalca*. The enemy numbered at least thirty thousand men, most entirely naked, the rest clothed in cotton weaved in various colors and in plumage, carrying only wooden swords, clubs, and bows and arrows for arms. Seeing the hot-headed appearance of the savages as they slowly approached them, the Spanish cavalry skirmishing here and there and drawing the enemy into battle, often pretending to flee, and the infantry also seeing such flight, the enemy began to take heart and chase hard on the Christians' heels.[6]

## DEFEAT OF THE PERUVIANS

Pizarro ordered twenty-two artillery pieces to open fire, which stunned these poor people, who had never even seen horses, let alone heard artillery thundering, which cut more than seven thousand barbarians down. The others took to flight by the hills and dales, [642v] hotly pursued by the Spaniards, who killed two times as many that day and the next, sparing neither the strong nor the weak, neither old nor young,

---

6. Thevet's account omits the dramatic confrontation, found in a number of sources, between the Dominican Vicente Valverde and Atahuallpa before the battle of Caxamalca. According to Benzoni, who is noted for his hostility to Spanish behavior in the New World, Atahuallpa, after looking at Valverde's Bible "laughed and said:—'This says nothing to me,' so [he] threw it on the ground; whence the monk took it back again and immediately called out with a loud voice,—'Vengeance, vengeance, Christians, for the gospels are despised and thrown on the ground! Kill these dogs, who despise the law of God.'" *History of the New World*, ed. and trans. Smyth, 179.

## CAPTURE OF ATABALIPA

saving only Atabalipa and six others of his council, who were taken, well beplumed, in a tent, near a stream named Chelcaiou in their dialect. I know this by learning it from a Spaniard in Seville, who had been there, and wounded twice by arrows in the battle.

## PRESENTS GIVEN BY ATABALIPA TO PIZARRO

Pizarro, seeing that he had the upper hand, approached Atabalipa and, having put a hand on his shoulder, as a sign of friendship, said several very gracious things to him. When he had finished, the captured king pulled covertly two fine pearls, large and round as a plum, from his breast, along with two emeralds, one carved as a bell and the other oval of unbelievable value and gave them to the conqueror, in order to remain in his good graces and to save his life. He promised him boundless riches and tried by all means to satisfy Spanish greed, which saw no greater goal than to enrich themselves. Now this Cacique Atabalipa did all he could in Pizarro's behalf: even though he had paid the equivalent of ten millions in pure gold in ransom, which he had brought from all the lands he possessed, to the point that they had to take the golden idols from the temples.[7]

## CRUELTY DEMONSTRATED TOWARD ATABALIPA

This did him very little good, in as much as, a few days after his capture, he was bound and gagged for three whole days and nights against a tree like the most miserable creature in the world, in order to make him confess if he knew of any other riches. Upon which, not fearing death, he insulted Pizarro a thousand times, assuring him that the God whom Pizarro worshipped and professed to be so just, would shortly punish him and his brother as well. So it happened,

7.   There are many descriptions of Atahuallpa's ransom. William H. Prescott claimed it had no parallel in all history (*History of the Conquest of Peru*, 1:454, 453–55, n.4). He also described the ransom as consisting of enough gold to fill a room twenty-two by seventeen feet to a height of nine feet, and enough silver to fill a smaller room twice (1:422). For more details, see "Report on the Distribution of the Ramsom of Atahuallpa, certified by the Notary Pedro Sancho," in *Reports on the Discovery of Peru*, ed. and trans. C. R. Markham (London, 1872), 131–43.

for Francisco Pizarro was killed shortly thereafter, and his brother Ferrand was decapitated in the same country.[8]

### Atabalipa strangled

Pizarro's lieutenants were in disagreement over whether to put this king to death or send him to the emperor Charles V, but they decided to strangle him, which was done at night, after he was sentenced by some bishops and monks, out of fear that his people might rescue him. A Moorish slave strangled him with the chord from an arquebuss.[9]

### Atabalipa was not burned

I am well aware that some have written that he was burned alive,[10] a silly thing of them to write, as the one who was present has assured me. All he was charged with was putting his brother Guiescart to death and stealing his country by invading it.[11]

### Praise of Atabalipa

This late king was a great judge, and he had built and enriched many sumptuous temples a dozen or so years before his death. Pizarro allowed his body to be carried honorably by his friends and supporters to be buried in the [643r] resting place of his father and mother.

8.   Gonzalo Pizarro, not Ferrand, was decapitated.

9.   Various sources describe the death of Atahuallpa differently. Details can be found in *History of the Conquest of Peru*, Appendix 10: "Contemporary Accounts of the Execution of Atahuallpa," 2:480–85.

10.   We have found no written account of the burning of Atahuallpa. The Spaniards changed the method of execution from burning to strangulation because Atahuallpa converted to Christianity just before his death.

11.   In addition to those given here by Thevet, the charges against Atahuallpa included idolatry, adultery, and an attempt to incite insurrection against Spanish rule. For details of Atahuallpa's trial, see *Reports on the Discovery of Peru*, ed. and trans. Markham, 102–5, n.3.

## WIVES AND CHILDREN OF ATABALIPA

Even though he had two hundred twenty living wives when he was taken, he had but two daughters, almost grown. He died at the age of fifty-two.[12] I am well aware that a few ignoramuses have described his life in a way entirely at odds to the truth, boasting of having been in these lands, where I know they never were: among others one named Girolamo Benzoni, as he boasts in a book printed at Geneva,

## HISTORY OF THE NEW WORLD

which, I am sorry to have to say, was enriched with several contributions from master Urbain Chauveton, such as the brief story of Francisco Lopéz de Gomarro [Gómara], Spaniard.[13]

## PORTRAIT OF ATABALIPA

So much for the history of Atabalipa, of whom I reproduce the portrait here, as I have brought it with several others I keep with me because they are rare and precious. Moreover, it is very disagreeable that some dolts have taken offense that Pizarro allowed those handling Atabalipa's body to give him a decent burial.[14]

### PIZARRO TO BE PRAISED FOR HAVING ALLOWED THE PERUVIANS TO BURY THEIR KING ATABALIPA

I shall not deign to recall here the perfidious act which this Spaniard had already performed by not having kept his word to this poor Infidel, after having received such a great and excessive ransom from him. I shall rebut what they say sufficiently with examples from the Pagans themselves who, after the death of their enemies, hon-

12. Francisco Xeres, Pizarro's secretary, wrote that Atahuallpa was about thirty years old when he died. Ramusio, *Terzo volume*, f.326v.

13. Thevet refers here to Urbain Chauveton's French translation of Benzoni's *History* (1579). He also appears to be implying, correctly in this case, that Benzoni's work borrowed much from Gómara, *Historia general*.

14. We have been unable to identify the "dolts" to whom Thevet refers; perhaps this is simply a rhetorical device allowing him to demonstrate his knowledge of Roman history.

ored them in burial, recognizing with the Orator Demosthenes that, though all men be more or less subject to envy and ill will while they live, they are exempt at least after their death. This is the reason which moved so many excellent and brave generals to treat their enemies more humanely after their death than they would have done during their lives.

### PAGAN GENERALS HONORED THEIR ENEMIES
### WITH BURIAL AFTER THEIR DEATH

*A propos* we read that Hannibal (recognizing that it is preferable, as they say, to kiss a dead enemy than fight a live one, in as much as the dead [*mort*] enemy never bites [*mord*]), sworn enemy of Rome to the death, having defeated and killed the Consul Caius Flaminius near the lake of Perusa, with fully fifteen thousand of his soldiers, took great care to recover the body of the dead Consul, to whom he gave honorable burial,[15] in the same pious way that he did to Tiberius Gracchus, whom he surprised in the ambush of the Luccans: Marcus Marcilius and Emilius Paulus defeated in the battle of Cannae. The Consul Lucus Cornelius was gentle in this way when he had the body of Hannon, general of the Carthaginian armies, taken from his tent and taken ceremoniously to be buried. If therefore the pagan Generals, permitted, purchased, and pursued the funerals of their deadly enemies without fear of reproach, what objection could there be to Pizarro's having released Atabalipa's body to his people, to honor it with funeral rites? In the same way as there are some who are shocked that Pizarro allowed friends of this king Atabalipa [643v] to bury him, others allowed themselves to invent the most bizarre funeral it is possible to imagine for him.

---

15.   Thevet's information about Hannibal burying Caius Flaminius (but without the parenthetical remark) and Lucius Cornelius burying Hanon comes from Guichard, *Funerailles*, 15.

### ERROR OF GUICHARD, AND OTHERS ON THE SUMPTUOUSNESS OF PERUVIAN FUNERALS

In the mold of a like fiction (for that is all I can think about it), the Munsterian Reformer [Belleforest] and after him the Doctor of funeral ceremonies Guichard told the lie that they revealed on the sumptuousness of Peruvian tombs and burials, as the well-disposed reader will discover on the first clear day. In the first place, his ninth chapter of his third book on funerals is too obviously a Gargantuan tale, when he builds a store of mummies in hollows of the high mountains of the land and kingdom of Cusco, Tombes, and Colao, and toward that end send their drug peddlers into these countries and mountains which are the most exposed to the North wind.[16] I have no wish here to belabor them for their inexperience, in as much as I know that neither Guichard nor his author [Belleforest] have traveled as far as I have. I shall merely ask them to ask Spanish merchants who deal at the Lyon market-fairs to enquire whether any of these good mummies are found by these drug peddlers in these parts and in that case (otherwise I presume that, had he known, he would never have dared publish such a lie) he will learn that there is no trace, any more than there is in his Lagnieu.

### TOO GREAT SUMPTUOUSNESS IMPUTED TO THE TOMB OF THE KING OF CUSCO BY GUICHARD AND FRANCISO LOPÉZ [DE GÓMARA]

Even more ridiculous is the foolishness which he takes from his Benzoni that the Peruvians bury many gold and silver works along with the most beautiful and best beloved of their wives, servants, utensils, bread, wine, and other comestibles so that they could eat and drink until they arrive in the other world. A single word is all that is needed to make the falseness of such a tale obvious. Good God, where would they have dug up such wine to give to the dead? for,

---

16. Ibid., bk. 3, ch. 9, "Des funerailles & sepultures des peuples des terres descouvertes de nostre temps, ausquelles on a donné le nom de Nouveau monde, & d'Indes Occidentales ou Amerique" (437–66, esp. 437–38). Guichard himself (437 n.a) cites François de Belleforest, *Histoire universelle* (Paris, 1570) as his source. Thevet's reference to a "Gargantuan tale" may have been inspired by Rabelais, *Gargantua and Pantagruel*, bk. 5, ch. 38, "The Marvellous Emblems on the Temple Pavement."

if a vineyard with ripe grapes can be found in the continent of Peru and land of America from one pole to the other, Thevet concedes to Guichard, who might with his authors have confused wine with an entirely different liquor, or indeed with the one Peruvian nobles use in place of wine. As for the tomb of the king of Cusco, which Guichard, following the Spaniard Lopéz [de Gómara] in chapter 124 of his History of the Indies,[17] shows placed in the middle of a chapel of which the floor was paved entirely with gold, it must be entered on the list with the others, and even though the building is vividly imagined, it is no more solid than the hope given by those who are accustomed to promise mountains of gold.

17. Guichard, *Funerailles*, 438, n.c; chap. 124 of Gómara, *Historia general*, is titled "Calidades y costumbres del Cusco" (2:37–38).

## MOTZVME, ROY DE MEXIQVE.

### Chapitre. 142.

TOVT ainsi qu'vn haut & eminent edifice, tant plus il est esleué, faict vn plus grãd, plus lourd & plus desolé soubre-saut, dés qu'il vient à boule-uerser: aussi tant plus haut sont montés les Princes, sils viennent à tresbucher, c'est alors qu'ils font plus piteux & plus horrible esclat que sils n'eussent esté nichés si haut. L'experience iustifiera de mõ dire, & notamment le present discours, qui representera vn abbregé de l'estat de la magnificence & richesse de ce Roy, qui fut en fin telle-

[This portrait of Montezuma provides a good example of Thevet's concern for authenticity. Lacking any knowledge of his actual appearance, Thevet tried to construct an accurate portrait by using details from the illustrations in the *Codex Mendoza*. Joppien gives a detailed comparison of the Montezuma portrait and the *Codex* in "Etude de quelques portraits," 128–31, and figs. 2, 5–8.]

# Montezuma,
# King of Mexico

Just as a tall and imposing building makes a more resounding and impressive crash when it collapses, the higher it is built in the first place, so a prince, the higher he rises, becomes the more pitiable and noteworthy if ever he falls than if he had never risen so high in the first place. Experience will prove the truth of what I am saying, particularly the present discourse, a summary of the magnificence of this king, who was finally so [644v] abandoned by fortune that, reduced to the calamity of prison, he was stoned to death by his own subjects.

### Montezuma's riches

The infinity of his riches was such that it is impossible to give a reliable accounting of them, at least without great difficulty. There are in fact many who have been so struck by the multitude of these riches that they did not dare try to count them, since he possessed so many statues of gold and silver, so precious that their quantity and quality defy belief. Moreover, the statues were of such fine workmanship that, even though the Indians did not have the convenience of iron tools, still they were so unbelievably well crafted that the finest sculptor or jeweler could not only not do better, but could not do as well.

### Montezuma's clothes and his portrait

His clothing of feathers was so subtly woven that it would be impossible to do better with wax or with silk embroidery. I have already described the extent of his dominions in sufficient detail in my Cosmographie:[1] there have been Princes with more territory than he held, if we measure Empires by the yard, but there have been precious few to whom he would have had to yield in magnificence of buildings, defenses, palaces, gardens of earthly delights, nor in household furnishings, which were so pridefully sumptuous that all one saw there was gold, silver and precious stones. As for the ostentatious plenty of his meals, I do not believe that there has ever been a prince with such unnecessary bounty as this king. His meal was fit for an ambassador, in that both flesh and fish were served, in all the varieties available there. It was expressly forbidden to bring back dishes that had ever been served to him; they had to be refashioned anew. He changed clothes four times a day, and never put back on what he had once taken off.

### Mexicans do not dare gaze on their king's face

He held himself so far removed from the normal run of men that none who entered the palace dared look at him, and he showed himself outside only rarely. If he did happen to go outside, none was so foolhardy as to raise his eyes to look upon the king's face. Those who did meet him outside had to turn their face to the side so as not to see him.

### How the king of Borneo spoke to those with whom he had business

In much the same way the king of Borneo spoke only to his wife and children. When he had to speak to others, he did so by speaking to a member of his court through a blow- pipe through a hole in the wall, as he did to the Ambassador from his most Catholic majesty, as we

---

1. Mexico is covered in Thevet's *Cosmographie universelle*, 2:bk. 22, chaps. 14–17, English trans., Schlesinger and Stabler, *André Thevet's North America*, 172–215.

learn in the histories of the Indies.[2] He traveled in a litter carried by
men who had to comport themselves with such humility that they
had to carry this heavy load with bare shoulders and bare feet. I am
sorry [645r] to have gone on at such length on the greatness of this
King [Montezuma], who was nonetheless unable to parry the heavy
blow which fell upon his head[3] and brought him to a pitiful end, even
though he was as wily and astute as any man. He knew how to play
a double game to the hilt, as he showed the Spaniard Cortés, whom
he tried to prevent by every means at his disposal from entering his
territory.

### MEANS BY WHICH MONTEZUMA SOUGHT TO PREVENT CORTÉS FROM ENTERING HIS LANDS

There were no presents, offers, nor trades that Montezuma failed
to try since, as we saw from the outcome, he was caressing a man
whose corpse he hoped to kiss (as we say). As soon as he learned
of the Spanish fleet under Cortés's command which had landed in
the Province of Tascallecal [Tascalteca], out of fear that they pressed
too close upon him, he sent four of his leading citizens to ask for
an alliance with them, and to promise that he would be a faithful
subject and loyal vassal of the King of Spain. The song ended on
a somewhat different note, however: he begged them not to enter
his dominions. Seeing that his prayers were unavailing, he set an
ambush for them between the cities of Tascallecal and Curultelcal
[Cholula?], and sent ambassadors to ask them to take this road in
order to make their wishes known to him. Had not Cortés been
informed of Montezuma's perfidy, the Spaniard would have fallen
unawares into the trap which the Mexicans hoped to spring on him.
Montezuma had hoped to take full advantage of the ambush, but
what he ended up doing was giving the Spaniard ample matter for
reflection, on how to temporize so that he could later give this wily
fox as good as the fox had hoped to give. The latter, seeing that
he could not hope to save himself by playing the lion, he sought

2. Cf. Gómara, *Historia general*, chap. 95, "De Siripada, rey de Borney," 1:227–31, esp. 229.

3. Here Thevet may be referring to the manner of Montezuma's death.

instead treacherously to entrap the Spaniard by the handsome offers of humility, devotion, favors and gratitude which he vowed to the king of Spain. This was not the end of the story, though, for all these wily and tricked out offers failed utterly to blind Ferdinand who, having discovered the trickery used by Montezuma, proved the truth of the old proverb, that guile only begets greater guile.

### CORTÉS SEIZES MONTEZUMA'S PERSON

Under the authority of his sovereign lord, Cortés made his way to Montezuma, and learned from him all there was to know of the secrets of Mexico. When he saw that the time was ripe to seize a person who could resist and make trouble for him, Cortés locked him up nobly in prison: on the pretext that a few Spaniards had been foully murdered by *Qualpopaca*, who was executed with his accomplices by Montezuma's order. The execution did the poor Montezuma no good, though: even though the criminals formally denied during their trial that he had anything to do with it, when they understood that they were to be burned at the stake, they placed the blame [645v] on their king, who was apprehended, and died in the way I have described above in the life of Ferdinand Cortés. I am well aware that there are those who, in order to besmirch the Spaniard's reputation, maintain that only his ambition and avarice toward Montezuma caused him to forge this crime, and that on the contrary the latter had acted with all the courtesy and nobility imaginable toward Cortés and his company, to the point of sending his own brother to earn his good will. They, however, do not know the character of this Mexican who, having to deal with one wilier than he, was completely bested. Cortés crushed him so completely that he served alone as a target for his enemies. Thus, in a very short time, ended the glory of such a great and feared prince; the subjects who had earlier not dared gaze upon his visage for the respect they bore him did not hesitate to stone him unto death.

### ERRORS ON THE PART OF F DE BELLE FOREST

As for the description of the city of Themistitan and of the kingdoms under Montezuma's rule, I have already treated them at sufficient length in my Cosmographie.[4] I have nonetheless to digress in order to chase from the forest of Munster [Belleforest] newly recreated the tale that they sell small castrated dogs in Themistitan which the Mexicans fatten in order to eat later.[5] This custom, according to him, is seen nowhere but in Themistitan (which is at 272 degrees of longitude and 18 of latitude). This poor chap allowed himself to be bamboozled by the first tall tales that charlatans managed to breath in his ear. Equally well-founded is the association which he and a few others make with the Canary Islands and the multitude of dogs one finds there.[6] All this is just as far-fetched as the sacrifices which he imputes to Mexicans and Brazilians, so cruel that fathers do not scruple to sacrifice their own sons, as the sons do their fathers. To write this is really to take gargantuan liberties with the truth.[7]

4.   See note 1.

5.   Belleforest, *Cosmographie universelle*, 2:col. 2141.

6.   Ibid., 2:col. 2027.

7.   We have not found these references in Belleforest.

## De A. Theuet , Liure VIII.

### NACOL-ABSOV , ROY DV PROMON-
*toire des Cannibales.* Chapitre. 145.

Evx qui ont prins plaisir de fureter les causes des guerres, qui pour le iourdhuy tinta-
marrent les Estats de ce monde, ont pour la
plus-part ( comme l'on dit) rompu l'anguille
au genouil, pour autāt qu'ils n'ont pas regar-
dé plus loin que leur nés, & se sont contan-
tés sils pouuoyent coucher seulement par
escrit que les Princes s'entrequereloyent par
ambition ou par hayne particuliere, dont ils s'entre-haissoyent l'vn
l'autre, mais quant ils liront l'histoire de ce Nacol-absou, faudra bien,

*Cause des guerres.*

# Nacol-absou, King of the Promontory of the Cannibals

Those who took pleasure in finding the causes of the wars which are now resounding throughout our world have, for the most part (as we say) reached for the moon, in as much as they have refused to look past the end of their noses,

### Cause of wars

and have been content to write that Kings quarrel out of ambition, or a private hatred which two may nurse for each other. They shall have to [650v] change their tune for a higher one, recognizing that such bitterness comes from the depravity of human nature, which sowed in our hearts the fiery sparks which light the fires of discord and dissension among them. For this reason philosophers who preferred dumb animals to men were right.

### Man in general is worse than the beasts

One seldom sees animals of the same species eating each other, hence the ancient proverb, that it is indeed alarming to see wolves devouring each other. This ought to restrain the rage of those who, under the guise of "humanity," are worse, more cruel and heartless, toward their fellows worse than wolves would be, however fierce and wild they may be. If ever some wolves take it into their heads to attack their own kind, others rush in to separate them and stop them from tearing each other to pieces. To deny that a few beasts are exempt from this accord would be to fly too obviously in the face of the truth but, the closer one looks, the more obvious it becomes that the exception is by virtue of the proximity of these animals to men, who teach them to mistreat each other in the way that we see cats, dogs, horses, birds and other animals fall on each other and tear and claw at each other with claw, fang and beak. The cruelty and ferocity of all the animals gathered together does not approach the fondness for tearing each other to shreds of human beings, formed in likeness of the Almighty.[1] I am well aware that we are used to saying that familiarity engenders the storms of discord so common among the world of men. I should be sorry to call this truth into doubt, but to lay all the blame for our enmity for each other at its feet would also be to hide some of the truth of the present discourse, which will show us a Kinglet [*Roitelet*] of the Cannibals[2] who tried to ambush and kill us, as he had done a month before to two Portuguese ships.

### NACOL-ABSOU'S CRUELTIES

After the death of the Portuguese, he and his men made a nice stew of them as is fully recounted in my Cosmographie.[3] The occasion which caused him to do this has been diversely remarked by many, who gabbled on about it as their fancies dictated. Some have fixated on the fact the the Spaniards had committed ten thousand crimes, depradations, and indignities, of every description wherever they planted their flag. They suppose, therefore, that this Barbarian, on the assumption that anybody approaching his lands planned to act

1.   Thevet's analyses of the causes of violence here is typical of sixteenth-century authors, who often compared the behavior of wild animals favorably with that of humans. For examples, see J. R. Hale, "Sixteenth-Century Explanations of War and Violence," *Past and Present* 51 (May 1971):3–26, esp. 15.

2.   Sturtevant has identified Nacol-absou as a Potiguara, a people who occupied a region north of the Tupinamba between the Parnaíba and Paraíba rivers. See "First Visual Images of Native America," in *First Images of America*, ed. Chiappelli, 1:417–54, esp. 437; and John Hemming, "The Indians of Brazil in 1500," in *The Cambridge History of Latin America*, ed. Leslie Bethell, 5 vols. (Cambridge, U.K., 1984), 1:119–43, esp. 133 and map on 121.

3.   We have been unable to find it. A less spectacular version, however, appeared in *Singularitez*: "A little before our arrival, the Americans who claimed to be our friends had captured a small ship full of Portuguese which was still near the shore. It was taken in spite of all the resistance they put up, with their cannons and all, and all the men were eaten except for a few whom we bought upon our arrival." Paris, 1558 ed., f.74v, see *Singularités*, ed. Lestringant, 84–85.

like Spaniards there, acted to prevent them from discovering and catching a scent of how rich, fertile and pleasant his country was, out of fear that they would immediately [651r] wish to land, settle, and set up housekeeping there. Others impute his actions to some fierce and Barbaric inhumanity which made this gallant man so touchy that he could not abide any one coming anywhere near his territory without trying to put the newcomer under his control. This last confirms what I said at the outset, that the enmity between men is so natural that, even when they have not had contact with each other, the natural corruption with which their sinful natures smears them to take into their bellies causes them to do their best to devour each other. You can see the tiger-like cruelty[4] of this Barbarian who, after having seized sixty-seven Portuguese from these two ships by devious and subtle means, subjected them to such horrible and execrable butchery that the very Cannibals could not help themselves from so grumbling about it that some Spaniards heard about it after casting anchor there. For his part, Nacol-absou retreated to the border of the Promontory [Cabo Santo Agostinho], out of his fear that these Foreigners might attack him and seize his kingdom to avenge the ambush and death of their Christian brothers.

### THE PROMONTORIES OF CANNIBALS AND OF GOOD HOPE THE BEST KNOWN OF THE GREAT SEA

This Promontory, along with that of the Lion in High Ethiopia,[5] commonly known as [Cape] of Good Hope, is the best known of the Great Sea. They are 1,704 leagues apart: the Promontory of the Lion is at 34 degrees south Latitude, while that of the Cannibals is at 340 degrees and zero minutes of longitude and thirty degrees of latitude,

---

4.   Thevet's characterization here is reminiscent of Konyan Bebe's declaration: "I am a tiger" (jaguar?) in Staden's *Warhaftig Historia*, f.miir (English trans., *Hans Staden: The True History of His Captivity*, 1557, ed. and trans. Malcolm Letts [New York, 1929], 110). Michael Palencia-Roth argues convincingly that Thevet knew, and used, Staden's work. See "Cannibalism and the New Man of Latin America in the 15th- and 16th-Century European Imagination," *Comparative Civilizations Review* 12 (Spring 1985):16–17.

5.   In *Singularitez*, Thevet wrote that pilots called the Cape of Good Hope the Lion of the Sea "because it was so feared, for it was so large and difficult of passage" (Paris, 1558 ed., f.40v; see also f.119r for a similar statement).

as my Insulaire shows at length and in full.[6] Even though this land of Cannibals is fertile, and the climate is gentle, nonetheless it spawns some of the most fierce, as well as the most skilled in combat, of any men on this earth. So much so that sailors who anchor and put ashore in the harbors and rivers of this land put themselves in great and obvious peril, unless they are astute and well-protected. I can bear witness myself, having experienced the fury of these brutes, who hunted me so closely that it was all I could do to escape with my life,[7] so hungry are these curs not only for Christian or foreign flesh, but even for that of their neighbors and compatriots. When they manage to seize some of the latter, Heaven knows how they celebrate their execrable meal. Those who live on the islands are not as inhuman as those who live on dry land, though the best of them is worth little more than nothing. There is no islet without its king, and many [islands] have two or three if they are large enough.

### Blunders perpetrated by historians of America

I find myself obligated to correct the stupidity of those who write too rashly [651v] that when these people eat one another and when they seize children, that they castrate them to fatten them, as we do with capons and goats.[8] I have no wish to give them the lie by the proof I could produce to the contrary of what I myself have seen when I was in those parts, vastly preferring to beat them with what everyone knows, that a castrated man is usually feeble, flaccid, frumpled, and foul-tempered, so that the reason that they impute to the Cannibals for castrating their enemies turns out to be false, ridiculous, and absurd, and it follows that everything based on such an illegitimate reason is all the further removed from the truth. As

6.   "Grand Insulaire," 1:f.245.

7.   We doubt the truth of this story on the basis that Thevet made no mention of it in *Singularitez*, written immediately after his return from the New World.

8.   Thevet here criticizes Belleforest's statement: "and taking some children of neighboring tribes, they castrate them and fatten them, like capons, then kill them and eat them" (*Cosmographie universelle*, 2:col. 2072). As noted in the Introduction, Thevet and Belleforest were contemporary—and rival—cosmographers; neither missed an opportunity to denigrate the other's work and reputation. The information on castrated children, however, is found in Spanish sources to which both authors had access.

is what they bruit falsely about the old, whom they kill and salt, so that they can use them to lard fish, fowl, and other foods. When I read such absurdities, I recall the proverb which recounts that it is licit to lie to those who come from afar, but the proverb applies only if there is no one to persuade the stranger to look up when he stumbles against the barrier of truth. I shall leave these delightful yarn-spinners here and return to our tale of Nacol-absou who, as he always coveted that which belonged to others, planned to seize a fort which some Spaniards had erected by a fresh-water stream. After killing many of the garrison, however,

## DEATH OF NACOL-ABSOU

he was unable to prevent his own death from a musket shot so well aimed that the most pressing task left to him was to go looking for the morrow of All Saints' Day. His body was born into the fort, and his head to Seville, as proof positive that he would no longer be undertaking his ravages on Christians.

## PORTRAIT OF NACOL-ABSOU

His portrait, moreover, which I represented for you here, was modeled after one made by a painter from Maiorca, in which he held a kind of spear which he handled expertly.[9] Though some savages carry flat green stones in their lower lips [?], of which I own some myself, the Cannibals and inhabitants of the Orelane [Orellana] and Vrabe [Uraba] rivers and others wear long ones, in the way you see them depicted here in the visage of this kinglet, who wore three long stones, at least half a foot long, not that they were precious, since this fourth part of the world which we have just discovered boasted no rubies, diamonds, emeralds, sapphires, nor Turquoise,[10] unless they were carried there from the provinces of China, Malaca, Cathay, the Mollusk Islands, or other countries of the East Indies in Asia.

9.   There is a different portrait of a "Roy des Canibales" in *Cosmographie universelle*, 2:f.955v (see fig. 2 of this volume).

10.   Brazil, of course, turned out to be rich in mineral deposits, including emeralds and gold, which was discovered late in the seventeenth century.

## PARACOVSSI, ROY DE PLATTE.

### Chapitre. 147.

Son pour-traict.

'A y trois chofes à obferuer principalement en la fuite de ce difcours. La premiere fe ra-portera au pourtraict de ceft argenté Prince. La fecóde fera touchant ce, qui eft remarqua-ble en fa vie. Et la derniere de quelques fingu-larités qui font à obferuer en cefte contrée, où il a commandé. Quant à fon effigie ie l'ay re-couuré d'vn matelot, qui fit le voiage d'icelle riuiere de mon temps, tirée au naturel, & fuiuant la façon qu'il auoit accouftumé d'eftre habillé, portant vne pierre bien polie au trauers

SSSSf iiij

[Hulton and Quinn, *The Work of Jacques Le Moyne de Morgues*, have identified similarities between Thevet's portraits of the "King of Plata" and Paraousti Satouriona and figures of Timucua Indians in the foreground of Theodore de Bry's illustration "The Formation and Equipment of Outina's Forces" in the second part of *America*.* Because the latter appeared only in 1591, seven years after *Vrais pourtraits*, Hulton and Quinn suggest that Thevet may have had access to original Le Moyne drawings known today only through the de Bry engravings, and that the former served as the bases of these two portraits.** Furthermore, the statements about the king wearing a well-polished stone in his nose, having the ends of his fingers cut off, and wearing plumage on his head indicate that Thevet was actually describing the portrait accompanying the Paraousti Satouriona chapter, and that the two were accidentally transposed.]

---

\* Hulton, et al., *The Work of Jacques Le Moyne de Morgues*, 1:208, 217; 2:pl. 106. Specifically, the right-hand figure in the foreground is associated with the "King of Plata," and the left-hand figure with Paraousti Satouriona.

\*\* Cf. Lestringant's review of Hulton's work in *Bibliothèque d'Humanisme et Renaissance* 42 (1980):776–78; and Sturtevant, "First Visual Images," 451, n.45.

# Paracoussi,
# King of the Platte

I have three main things to observe in what follows. The first will concern the portrait of this gilded prince.[1] The second will take up what is remarkable in his life. And the last will be a few remarkable things which can be seen in the land he ruled.

## His portrait

As for his likeness, drawn from life and showing his normal dress, I got it from a sailor, who made the trip up that river in my time.[2] He wore a well polished stone in his [656v] nose as a sign of having killed many, as American Kings cut their bodies front and back after having bloodied themselves in the murder of their enemies. And his body was clothed in the skins of beasts, which will not seem strange to those who will have, if not seen with their own eyes, at least read or heard the true discourse of those who tell us that they are clothed in skins which are not tanned or dressed. As for me, I can attest that this is the case, having not only seen these skins on others, but having earlier used them myself. The ends of his fingers have been cut off, except the thumbs, for these poor people have made it a custom to cut off these extremities. Alongside the head is attached an excellent plume, looking like a local bird which these Barbarians call Hyona,

---

1. Although Thevet gives few details about his subject, he is probably describing a northern Tehuelche Indian. These natives of the Patagonian plains—the original "Patagonian giants"—inhabited the area from the Straits of Magellan to the Río Negro in southern Argentina, and European literature celebrated their great stature and strength.

2. We have found no written sources for the information Thevet presents in this paragraph.

which is really a pigeon in Persian.[3] If the copper had allowed me to do justice to the diversity of colors it has, I would have gladly included them, for the recreation of the Reader's eye.


## His heroic acts

The defeats which he inflicted on those who rashly dared try to seize his land or to put their noses where he had not invited them could bear witness to his valiant acts, since these people are jealous of their land. Many who kicked up a fuss have felt the full Patagonian weight of this giant, who seemed to want to pierce the very earth when he let fly a blow against one of his enemies. He pursued them so relentlessly that he never let up until he made them lose their land. I know well that some, embroidering the truth quite a lot, have tried to account for his success by attributing it to some secondary demon or other.[4] But if they had heard what afflictions Setebos[5] visited upon these Barbarians, I do not believe that they would deign to lie so impudently to denigrate this powerful and feared King.


## Plata River

As for the country where he ruled, all agree that it was a fertile land with many blessings, and that, because of the abundance of Pearls which gather in this river, it was called the Sun, Plate or Gilded river, in which enter the rivers which fall from the mountains of the Patagonian region, to wit *Mecoretas, Xanez, Caramagna, & Carcarama*, which however are not part of the Patagonian reign, but rather of that of *Chinca* [Chincha] & [Las] *Charcas*, which are under the power of Cusco.[6] It lies at thirty-three degrees and zero minutes of Southern latitude. It floods once a year.

3.   Although Thevet claimed to know twenty-eight languages and had been to the Middle East, his Persian deserted him here: *Fākhtah* is Persian for *pigeon*.

4.   The secondary demon to which he refers may be Cheleule, mentioned by Ramusio in his extract of Pigafetta's account (*Primo volume*, f.354v).

5.   Pigafetta used this Tehuelche word for great spirit or devil. Ibid., f.354.

6.   This information about the rivers also appears, verbatim, in Belleforest's *Cosmographie universelle*, 2:col. 2042.

## QVONIAMBEC.

*Chapitre.* 149.

**P**LVSIEVRS, qui entendent parler des mer-
ueilleuses singularités, que Dieu despartist
en ces pays, qui nous ont esté ny a pas fort
long temps descouuers, sont en bransle, s'ils
doiuent adiouster foy au rapport, qui en a
esté faict par ceux, qui ont voiagé par toutes
ces regions & contrées incogneües. Qu'il
n'y ait occasion d'estre rauy en non-pareil
esbahissemét on ne scauroit le nier, soit qu'ó prêne aduis aux choses,
qu'ils ont communes auec nous, qui, encores qu'elles ne soyent si

# QUONIAMBEC

Many who hear about the marvelous attractions which God scattered in these lands, which have been discovered not so very long ago, are in a dither over whether they ought to believe the report given by those who have traveled to these unknown regions and countries. No one can deny that there be reason to be ravished with unparalleled bewilderment, if we take note of the things they have in common with us which, though they not be as [661v] subtly worked out as European dexterity can refine, have nonetheless the basic nature to dazzle into admiration the most blasé. The latter will be all the more taken aback when they learn that the Americans are ahead of us in many things. I shall not mention the fertility and pleasantness of the country, although she provides all too much matter for marvelous astonishment, by virtue of the amenities God hands out in such plenty in these countries, whom he has endowed with such excellence that a few foolish ignorant people, who could not apprehend that the Almighty can make his sun shine on the bad as well as the good, have tried to render an accounting of the gifts of the Everlasting, who has watered the fourth part of the world with such benedictions. But this is to say little indeed of the blessings with which he has covered the natives of these areas over there who, deprived of the true Sun of justice, the clarity of which they could perceive only very indistinctly, were nonetheless crowned with precious qualities, belonging as much to the body as to the spirit.

## QUONIAMBEC SEEN BY THE AUTHOR

All I wish to adduce as proof of what I say is the fearsome Quoniambec, of whom I may speak since I have seen, heard, and looked him over at my leisure on the banks of the Ianaire river, under the Tropic of Capricorn at twenty-three and a half degrees from the Equator and sixty-six and a half from the South Pole, where my lord Villegaignon had us stop.[1] This is the mistake of the writer [Belleforest] who, perhaps basing his calculations on those of Léry or some other raconteur, tried to place it at twenty-three degrees from the South Pole. Since this man was remarkable among all the others of this country, as much for his height as for the eminence which made him stand out above the others, he was occasionally convoked by our leader, who spoke with him to discover what was to be sought and prized.[2] This half giant was tall, broad, and robust, and he knew how to use his strength so well that his chief occupation was overcoming his enemies and forcing them to obey him. I recall having written somewhere in my Cosmographie[3] that the man whose portrait I reproduce here as I brought it from those parts, wearing two green stones which I still have in a cupboard in his cheeks and one at the end of his chin[4]

1.   There is no good reason to doubt Thevet's assertion that he personally observed Quoniambec, who is almost certainly the Tamoio chief whom Staden identified as Konyan Bebe (*Warhaftig Historia*, ed. Letts, 78–81). On the identification of Quoniambec as Konyan Bebe, also see Lussagnet, *Les Français en Amérique*, 88–89, n.3; and Lestringant, "Myth," 37–60, esp. 39. We thank Frank Lestringant for bringing this article to our attention.

2.   Thevet's description of Quoniambe as a "European-style" monarch who held summit-meetings with Villegagnon is ethnologically inaccurate, but Lestringant has proposed that Thevet purposely created this image because it was "indispensible for the establishment of alliances with the new peoples and further for the installation of jurisdiction over their territories. The isolation of a unique figure which marvellously realizes the monarchic principle transposed into Indian chieftainship considerably simplifies the transactions because the key to domination rests in a single individual, easy to convert and to corrupt" ("Myth," 47–48). As Lestringant suggests (52), Thevet, who enjoyed the patronage of four French kings, tended to equate political relations between states with personal relations between monarchs. On the relationship between Quoniambec's size, strength, and status, "it is because Thevet has made a European-style monarch out of the war chief that he has to confer upon him an exceptional stature. In the absence of written laws and a fixed code of justice defining as well the modes of accession to power and the prerogatives of the sovereign, the only citeria to determine the royalty of the Indian chief are of a physical kind: athletic frame and impressive muscles bulging, contrary to all racial accuracy, on the arms and shoulders of Quoniambec" (44).

3.   Thevet's descriptions of Quoniambec in *Singularitez* (Paris, 1558 ed.), ff. 103–4 and *Cosmographie universelle*, 2:ff. 907v [incorrectly numbered 908], 923–25, 952r are in striking contrast to the one presented here. In *Vrais pourtraits* he omits references to Quoniambec's nakedness and cannibalism, emphasizing instead his great physical strength and other virtues.

4.   Tupinamba men of the Atlantic seaboard wore polished plugs of green jadeite in their

## MARVELOUS STRENGTH OF QUONIAMBEC

was so strong that he could have carried a barrel of wine in his arms without hurting himself, and that, in order to dazzle his adversaries, he took two great muskets which he had taken by force from a Portuguese ship, which shot a bullet as large as a tennis ball, [662r] and put them on his shoulders, turning the mouth of his cannons towards his enemies. As soon as he felt them approach, he ordered one of his men to fire the pieces. These discharged, he took others until he had made them scatter, then God knows how he mocked them.[5] A truly uncommon story [*Histoire*] but one which those with a nose for the truth will have no difficulty believing to be possible, in view of the size and strength of his body.

## REBUKE TO JEAN DE LÉRY

Nonetheless de Léry, who passes himself off as the fount of all knowledge on the new world, does not deign to believe that this savage could have carried these two pieces without burning himself or rather injuring his shoulders by their recoil.[6] I shall not deign to belabor him with experience, since I am well aware that he has not seen the man of whom we are speaking here, and that he would never make a fool of himself by speculating without the basis of experience that alone makes wise men of fools. He still cannot win the argument, since neither Léry nor any other could stand in for

cheecks and lower lips. Natives greatly prized such stones and carefully traded them from tribe to tribe. See John Hemming, "The Indians of Brazil" in *The Cambridge History of Latin America*, ed. Leslie Bethell, 5 vols. (Cambridge, U.K., 1984), 1:125). Compare this portrait with the one in *Cosmographie universelle* (fig. 1).

5.   See the description of Quoniambec's "ruse" in *Cosmographie universelle*, 2:f.952, with an illustration (fig. 3).

6.   This chapter provides an excellent example of the hostility between the Catholic Thevet and the Calvinist Léry. Indeed, Léry's account of his experiences in Brazil—*Histoire d'un voyage* (La Rochelle, 1578)—included a strong attack on Thevet's *Singularitez*, which he thought was full of lies about the reasons for the failure of Villegaignon's enterprise. In a lengthy preface, Léry vigorously attacked Thevet ("I am determined not merely to attack him by the way afterwards but, what is more, to assault him so violently that I shall shut his mouth") and especially ridiculed his account of Quoniambec. This chapter of *Vrais pourtraits* is Thevet's rebuttal, but Léry had the last (printed) word in his third edition (Geneva, 1585) in a reworked "Preface, monstrant Principalement, les erreurs & impostures de Thevet."

Figure 3. "Quoniambec's ruse"

Quoniambec; for this reason it is indefensible to say that this great king could not have done what I truthfully recounted about him. In order not to be too subtle or philosophical, I shall confine myself in my proof to Léry himself. I shall first suppose (without conceding the truth of what I am about to say) that he composed the books which are attributed to him from his domain in Sancerre, including the one on his voyage to America,[7] although all those who know him, among others my lord de l'Espine, who lived in those parts for twelve years, at the same time as Léry, cannot believe it. I could point to several pieces, parts, and portions which he took from the works of others[8] but, in order not to start a new incident, I shall be quite happy (under the charge written above) more or less to allow him the works he has appropriated for himself. On the additional understanding, which he can hardly refuse me, that he agree that a man who works with his hands like Léry is not well enough trained to put into writing of the sort of his discourses, most of which he had drafted by others. But, lest he believe that all I have to contradict him is the ineptitude of his profession, let us (please) see if he has not written something in his books several times more unbelievable than the story of Quoniambec.

### Léry's lies

I am very ashamed to have to take pen in hand to cudgel this liar, who so stuffed [662v] the few writings we have in his name with lies that those who are the least ill disposed toward him are forced to blush at the ravings, stupidities, and fantasies with which he thinks to reward those who spend their time reading his follies.

---

7. Thevet here refers to Léry's *Histoire memorable de la ville de Sancerre* (La Rochelle, 1574) as well as his *Histoire d'un voyage*. In the former, Léry described the seige of Sancerre, in which the Protestant defenders were reduced to starvation and forced to surrender.

8. Thevet is correct in his accusation. Léry borrowed materials from *Singularitez* for his *Histoire d'un voyage*. See Francisco Rodrigues Leite, "Jean de Léry, viajante de singularidades," *Revista do Arquivo Municipal de São Paulo* 108 (1946):23–112, and Bernard Weinberg, "Montaigne's Readings for 'Des Cannibales,'" *Renaissance and Other Studies in Honor of William Leon Wiley* (Chapel Hill, 1968), 264–79.

## LÉRY THE OYSTER

He was so crazy that, searching for the meaning of his name, he said that it means oyster in wild language, which is a manifest lie.[9] Even were it so, he is not so great as he makes out, in as much as he was an oyster locked up not between his two natural shells but in the fort of Coligny, where my lord Villegaignon kept him.

## LÉRY'S PRODIGIOUS TORTUSES

What shall we say about the prodigious tortuses he made in the tropics of such a frightening greatness that one could feed eighty persons (perhaps who had lost their appetite) and that a single shell could cover a house: I doubt that he meant a house for men, but rather for flies and such lesser beasts. Leaving these great whales, crocodiles one hundred feet long, and the rest of his fabulous tales,

## PRAISE-WORTHY VIRTUES OF QUONIAMBEC

I shall return to our Quoniambec, who was truly feared by the Margageas,[10] Portuguese, and his other enemies for the erectness and strength of his massive body. He was even more feared for his prudence which furnished him with such good grace that he took his enemies simultaneously with qualities of the lion and the fox. Moreover, as I wrote in the eighth chapter of the twenty-first book of my Cosmographie, he radiated several virtues, and was not among the most opposed to piety, accepting the immortality of the soul and taking pleasure at watching us in the exercise of our religion: he even fell to his knees with us when we prayed. He was the greatest boaster I have ever heard, who claimed to have defeated several thousand adversaries. His palace was in fact decorated and bordered with the heads of his enemies.

9.  *Histoire d'un voyage* (1578 ed.), 104–5, 310; and again in the Preface of the Geneva, 1585 edition.

10.  Thevet used this word, deriving from the Tupi *Markaja* (wildcat [*felix pardalis*]), to define, imprecisely, both the enemies of the Tupinamba and of the French in America. In popular French it became a synonym for *wild* or *barbaric* (Lussagnet, *Les Français en Amérique*, 17, n.1).

## Vases River

The territory subject to him in my day was very populous and bordered with mountains and rivers, which gave the name of Vases to the river in as much as traveling along in [it] one could see the cups of hills and rocks, naturally representing the form of vases made in either the classic or the modern way

## The bridge of pots

in the same way that the bridge in Revermont between Chastillon and Colonges is called the bridge of pots, in as much as, seeing the rocks shaped and fashioned like the vessels that they call oule from the Latin word *olla*,[11] you would think that the Rhone, which roils there at the foot of the Credote, boils like a pot, or tea kettle.

11.   Thevet's French and Latin here are correct; *olla* is an archaic word meaning *pot* or *urn*.

### PARAOVSTI SATOVRIONA, ROY DE LA
#### Floride.　　　Chapitre. 150.

A Floride eſt aſſés celebrée par les Hiſtoriés, qui ont deſcrit les ſingularités d'icelle, prenãs mire ſur la fleur, qu'elle porte en ſon frõt, qui, eſtant touſiours verde & eſpanouy e, à acquis à ceſte contrée le nom de Floride. Laquelle fut deſcouuerte en l'année mil cinq cens & douze, par vn Eſpaignol, nommé Iean Ponce de Leon, lequel, recerchant vne fontaine de Iouuence, deſcouurit la terre ferme de Floride, qui eſt vne pointe de terre, à la ſemblance de l'Italie, entrant en mer plus de cent lieuës : &

*Nom & deſcouuerte de la Flori-de, & en quelle eſte-uation elle eſt.*

[For the argument that this portrait may be based on a lost drawing by Jacques Le Moyne, and that it was accidentally transposed with the portrait of the "King of Plata," see the introductory remarks to the "King of Plata" chapter. Joppien, on the other hand, suggests that this portrait, together with that of Montezuma, is based on details of illustrations in the *Codex Mendoza*.[*]

---

[*]  Joppien, "Etude de quelques portraits," 131–32 and figs. 4, 8.

# Paraousti Satouriona, King of Florida

Florida is sufficiently famous through the efforts of Historians who have described her attractions,[1]

## Name and discovery of Florida,
### and how worthy she is

basing their accounts on the flower which she wears on her forehead which, since it is always in bloom, earned the name of Florida for this country. The country was discovered in the year 1512[2] by a Spaniard named Juan Ponce de Leon who, searching for a fountain of youth, discovered the land of Florida, which is a figure of land like Italy, stretching more than a hundred leagues into the sea, [663v] and the end is at twenty-five degrees of North latitude.

## The May River

This country is blessed with several islands and rivers, among which is the famous May River, both because it was discovered by Captain Jean Ribaud on the first of May,[3] which caused it to keep that name, and for the rarities which abound there. I shall not speak of the impiety and cruelty of which the Spaniards were guilty against this

---

1. Thevet used Laudonnière's *L'histoire notable de la Floride* for much of the information presented in this chapter.

2. Ponce de León discovered Florida in 1513, not 1512; see Henry Harrisse, *The Discovery of North America: A Critical, Documentary, and Historic Investigation* (Paris, 1892, repr. Amsterdam, 1961), 149–50, esp. 800–801. In his *Cosmographie universelle* (f.1001r), Thevet correctly stated that the name *Florida* derived from its discovery on Palm Sunday (*Pascua Florida*).

3. Jean Ribaud (Ribault) established the French colony at Charlesfort (Port Royal, S.C.) in 1562, and wrote *The Whole and True Discovery of Terra Florida* (London, 1563).

Norman Captain, particularly since such a tale would do nothing to cure such a bloody wound.[4]   In addition, Captain Gourgues[5] avenged this massacre adequately, by retaking Fort Caroline which Ribaud had built and named for his King Charles IX. Better that I concentrate on this May River, and on Paraousti Satouriona, who is called Satiroa,[6] a man of great courage who took on powerful adversaries,

## WARM WELCOME OFFERED BY SATOURIONA TO THE FRENCH

and who is otherwise remarkable for his hospitality to Captain Gourgues and his company. He so revered the French name that, when he first saw Gourgues's fleet, he ran immediately to them, crying, *Antipola, Antipola,* from fairly far away.[7] In every way he could think of, he gave them the warmest possible welcome with two of his children, as handsome people as can be found anywhere on earth. The eldest was named Atore, a man possessed of perfect beauty, prudence, and honest countenance, one of the most sweet, humane, and easy to deal with princes in this entire country. After they had exchanged greetings and gifts, this King told the French Captain what enemies he had, to wit Timagoa and Olata Ouaë Outina,[8] two very powerful

4.   A contemporary account of the Spaniards' mutilation of Ribaud's body is in La Popelinière's *Les trois mondes* (Paris, 1582), f.33v, and Thevet himself had described it in some detail in *Cosmographie*, f.1006r.

5.   Laudonnière included Dominique de Gourgues's account, "Le quatriesme voyage des Françis en Floride sous le Capitaine Gourgues, en l'an 1567," in his *L'histoire notable de la Floride,*, but Thevet did not use it for any material in this chapter. He apparently used Gourgues's name here—and throughout the chapter—to disguise the fact that his information came from Laudonnière's work, which he knew before it was published. Indeed, he used some of Laudonnière's materials for the Florida section of his *Cosmographie* as early as 1575, but suppressed any reference to them in order to pose as an authority on Florida. See Lestringant, "Les séquelles littéraires."

6.   This chief of the Satouriwa is usually called *Satouriona* or *Saturiba* in the sources.

7.   Again, Thevet uses Gourgues's name although his source is Laudonnière. This vocabulary is from *L'histoire notable de la Floride,* 69.

8.   Both the French and Spaniards commonly confused the names of localities with those of individuals. The Thimogona, or "Western Timuca," were allies and subjects of the Utina, whose lands extended westward from the St. Johns River; see Hulton, *Le Moyne,* 1:38 and Suzanne Lussagnet, *Les Français en Floride: Les Français en Amérique pendant la deuxième moitié du xvie siècle,* pt. 2, ed. C.-A. Julien (Paris, 1958), 93, n.1. Thevet's spelling of the two

Kings who had several allies: Olata himself had eight vassals,

### SOME KINGS OF FLORIDA

to wit Cadecha, Chilaly, Esclauou, Eucappe, Calanay, Onachaquara, Onittaqua, Moquoso, and Aquera, in addition to Molona and more than forty others who were allies and friends of his.[9] For his own part, he was not in bad shape at all to confront such a formidable force, as much for what he could do himself as for the support of thirty other parishes which were under his control, of which he was as sure as of himself, due as much to their obligations as allies, which reaffirmed their loyalty, as for the particular enmity which most bore toward Olata Ouaë Outina, especially *Onatehaqua* & *Houstagna*, powerful and rich lords, above all Onatehaqua, who ruled lands fertile in many of the necessities of life.[10] Satouriona made particularly sure of the loyalty of Potanou, a cruel [664r] warrior who had a hold over Olata because of the incursions he suffered because of the hard stones with which they tipped their arrows, which he [Olata] could only find in Potanou's lands.[11] As for his ten brothers, any injury done to Satouriona could not help but injure them as well, both because of their subordination, which obligated them to feel any injury done to their Lord and because of the fraternal relationship which bound them so closely together that a wound of one was immediately felt by all the others. All these forces unified together, though they were great and powerful, were not able to guarantee Satouriona the victory he sought over his enemies, who would have been loath to retreat before him. Nonetheless, when he saw the French fleet, he decided to resist Olata, more because of the natural prowess of a people hardened in combat

names varies throughout the chapter.

9.   Although Thevet says that Outina had eight "vassals," he actually names nine, following Laudonnière, *L'histoire notable de la Floride*, 89–90. Some of these names can be found on the Le Moyne map of Florida, discussed in Hulton, *Le Moyne*, 1:45–54.

10.   The Onatheaqua and Yustaga (Oustaca) tribes occupied land to the northwest of the Utina. The names may be found on the Le Moyne map of Florida.

11.   The Pontanou lived south and southwest of the Utina and are also on the Le Moyne map.

### Thunderbolt imputed to a cannonball

than because of the muskets the French carried, which so frightened these poor Savages that the Paracousi or Parousti Allycamany, when he saw the great destruction wrought by a thunderbolt which fell from the sky on August 29, sent six Indians to Captain Gourgues with some baskets of buckwheat, squash, and grapes, to make clear to him the eagerness of their Lord Allycamani to conclude a treaty of friendship and alliance with him. The messengers did find it strange, in view of their lord's loyalty to the French, that they had fired the cannonball toward his house, which burned a great number of fertile prairies, had even consumed water, and had come so near his house that he thought he had seen the fire from it. Be that as it may, assuming that Pagans were no more familiar with Jupiter's thunderbolts than these poor Floridians were with the terrible discharges of these fire-belching cannons, I cannot bring myself to believe that it was solely because of these mounted cannons that Satouriona valued the aid of the French. My reason is the hatred the king later felt toward the French, due to these thundering cannon

### Captain Gourgues's refusal to aid the king Satouriona

as well as to Captain Gourgues's subsequent refusal to escort Satouriona as he had promised in an attack against Thimogoa. Gourgues failed to take into consideration that Captain Vasseur, the Prince d'Ottigny and a few other Frenchmen had already discovered the treasures accumulated in the region, and had already brought some beautiful gifts, along with the assurance of more if they agreed to aid one of the lesser Kings, a vassal of the great Olata. This so tied the hands of the French that, after having played their double game for a long time, they were eventually forced to reveal to Satouriona their lack of eagerness to help him, which made him very angry. At this point, he decided to undertake [664v] the expedition against Thimogoa with ten other Paracoussis.

### Satouriona's rituals, before marching against Thimogoa

Before anything else, he had water brought to him. When it arrived, he cast his eyes to Heaven and began to speak of several things, giving evidence only of great anger. Having spoken for half an hour, he poured some of the water which he had in a vessel on the heads of the ten Paraoustis, and threw the rest, as if in anger, into a fire which had been built for the purpose.[12] After several other rituals, he embarked and made such good progress with his Almadies [canoes] that he arrived at the land of Thimoa at two the next day, before sunset.

### Satouriona gains victory over Thimoa

He made a terrible massacre of Thimoa's people. His men carried their heads off, and cut off the hair and a part of the scalp.[13] They led off twenty-four prisoners, of whom Satouriona had thirteen as his rightful escheat. As soon as Captain Gourgues heard about that, he sent a soldier to him to ask him for two of his prisoners.

### Challenge to Satouriona by Captain Gourgues

Satouriona refused very arrogantly, which caused Gourgues to enter Satouriona's chamber with twenty soldiers, without saluting or acknowledging him at all. After half an hour without saying a word, Gourgues said that the prisoners should be brought to him. After a while, Atore, son of Satouriona went to get them and brought them to Captain Gourgues, who took them with him. Satouriona, offended by the insult, made as if to avenge his honor but hid his evil intentions: he went on sending ambassadors to the French with

12.   This description is taken from Laudonnière, *L'histoire notable de la Floride*, 99. See also the De Bry engraving "Rituals Observed by Satouriona before setting out on a campaign against his enemies" in Hulton, *Le Moyne*, 2:pl. 103: described, 1:142–143.

13.   There are depictions of scalps and scalping in De Bry's engravings "How Outina's Soldiers treat the enemy dead" and "Trophies and Solemn Rituals when the enemy is conquered." Ibid., 2:pl. 107–8 and 1:144–45. See also James Axtell, *The European and the Indian: Essays in the Ethnohistory of Colonial North America* (Oxford, 1981), "The Unkindest Cut, or Who Invented Scalping? A Case Study " (16–35), and "Scalping: The Ethnohistory of a Moral Question" (207–41).

two baskets full of big squash. The leader of the French gave the Indians to understand that he wished to effect an accord between Thimogoa's people and the Paracousi Satouriona which could only turn to the latter's very considerable advantage, since, being allied with the Kings of the surrounding lands, this would give him free passage to attack Onathagua, his long-standing enemy whom he would not otherwise be able to attack. In addition, the great Olate was so powerful that Satouriona would only break and sap his own strength if he wished to confront him. But if they agreed, they could destroy all their enemies, and extend their control beyond the Southernmost rivers. In order to fulfill his promise, Gourgues dispatched Captain Vasseur, the Prince of Arlac and seven other soldiers toward Olate Ouaë Outina, to whom he sent his prisoners with the soldiers. Olate was very happy, all the more so that they were there to help him attack Parousti Ponano [Potanou], whom Olate charged at dawn with such fury with two hundred of his men and our French musketeers who were with him that he gained the victory.

THE END

# Select Bibliography

Adhémar, Jean. "André Thevet collectionneur de portraits." *Revue Archéologique* (1942–3): 41–54.

——. *Frère André Thevet, grand voyageur et cosmographe des rois de France au xvie siècle*. Paris, 1947.

——. *Inventaire du fonds Français: Graveurs du seizième siècle*. Paris, 1938.

Albuquerque, Afonso [Brás]. *Commentarios do grande Afonso Dalboquerque*. Lisbon, 1556. English trans., *The Commentaries of the Great Afonso Dalboquerque*, by Walter de Gray Birch. 4 vols. London, 1875–84.

Atkinson, Geoffroy. *Les nouveaux horizons de la Renaissance Française*. Paris, 1935.

Balmas, Enea. "Documenti inediti su André Thevet." In *Studi di letteratura storia e filosofia in onore di Bruno Revel*, 33–66. Florence, 1965.

Baudry, Jean. *Documents inédits sur André Thevet, cosmographe du roi*. Paris, 1983.

Belleforest, François de. *La cosmographie universelle de tout le monde*. 2 vols. Paris, 1575.

Bennett, Charles E. *Laudonnière and Fort Caroline: History and Documents*. Gainesville, 1964.

Benzoni, Girolamo. *Historia del Mondo Nuovo*. Venice, 1565 and 1572. English trans. and ed. W. H. Smyth, *History of the New World*. London, 1857. Reprint New York, 1970. Spanish trans., *La Historia del Mundo Nuevo*, with notes and introduction by Marisa Vannini de Gerulewicz, Estudio preliminar de León Croizat. Caracas, 1967.

Borba de Moraes, Rubens. *Bibliographia Brasiliana: A Bibliographical Essay on Rare Books About Brazil Published from 1504 to 1900.* Trans. Y. S. Untch. 2 vols. Amsterdam and Rio de Janeiro, 1958.

Brun, Robert. *Le Livre français illustré de la Renaissance.* Paris, 1969.

Céard, Jean. *La nature et les prodigies: L'insolite au 16e siècle, en France,* 282–89, 309–13. Geneva, 1977.

Chinard, Gilbert. *L'exotisme Américain dans la littérature Française au xvie siècle.* Paris, 1911.

Da Civezza, Marcellino. "André Thevet." In *Saggio di bibliografia geografia storica ethnografica Sanfrancescana,* 590–94. Prato, 1879.

De Jonghe, Edouard. "Thevet Mexicaniste." *International Congress of Americanists* (Stuttgart, 1906): 223–40.

Destombes, Marcel. "André Thevet (1504–1592) et sa contribution à la cartographie et à l'océanographie." *Proceedings of the Royal Society of Edinburgh,* sec. B. 72 (1971–72): 123–31.

Dexter, George. "Cortereal, Verrazano, Gomez, Thevet." In *Narrative and Critical History of America.* Ed. Justin Winsor. 8 vols. Boston and New York, 1884–89. Reprint New York, 1967, 4 (1884): 1–32.

Diaz del Castillo, Bernal. *Historia verdadera de la conquista de la Nueva España.* Madrid, 1632. English trans. *The True History of the Conquest of New Spain,* ed. Genaro García, trans. with introduction and notes by A. P. Maudslay. 5 vols. London, 1908–16.

Dickason, Olive P. *The Myth of the Savage and the Beginnings of French Colonialism in the Americas.* Edmonton, 1984.

Gaffarel, Paul. "André Thevet." *Bulletin de Géographie Historique et Descriptive* (1888): 166–201.

Gagnon, F-M. "Figures dans le texte. A propos de deux gravures dans Thevet." *Etudes Françaises* 14 (1978): 183–98.

Ganong, William F. *Crucial Maps in the Early Cartography and Place-Nomenclature of the Atlantic Coast of Canada,* with introduction, commentary, and map notes by Theodore E. Layng. Toronto, 1964.

Giovio, Paulo. *Gli elogi vite brevemente scritte d'huomini illustri di guerra, antichi et moderni.* Trans. Lodovico Domenichi. Venice, 1557.

Gómara, Francisco López de. *Historia general de las Indias.* Pt. 1 of *La Istoria de las Indias y conquista de Mexico.* Zaragoza, 1552. We have used the 2 vol. Madrid, 1922 edition.

————. *Historia de la conquista de México.* Pt. 2 of *La Istoria de las Indias y conquista de Mexico.* Zaragoza, 1552. We have used the English translation by L. B. Simpson: *Cortés: The Life of the Conqueror by His Secretary Francisco López de Gómara.* Berkeley, 1964.

Goulart, Simon, ed. and trans. *Histoire de Portugal.* Geneva, 1581.

Guichard, Claude. *Funerailles & diverses manieres d'ensevelir des Rommains, Grecs, & autres nations, tant anciennes que modernes.* Paris, 1581.

Guillemard, F. H. H. *The Life of Ferdinand Magellan and the First Circumnavigation of the Globe.* London, 1891.

Hakluyt, Richard. *The Principal Navigations Voyages Traffiques & Discoveries of the English Nation.* 2d ed. 3 vols. London, 1598–1600. Reprinted in 12 vols. Glasgow, 1903–5 and New York, 1965.

Hair, P. E. H. "A Note on Thevet's Unpublished Maps of Overseas Islands." *Terrae Incognitae* 14 (1982): 105–16.

Hulton, Paul, ed. *The Work of Jacques Le Moyne de Morgues: A Huguenot Artist in France, Florida and England.* Foreword, catalogue, and introductory studies by Paul Hulton, with contributions by D. B. Quinn, William C. Sturtevant, and William T. Stearn. 2 vols. London, 1977.

Joppien, Rüdiger. "Etude de quelques portraits ethnologiques dans l'oeuvre d'André Thevet." *Gazette des Beaux-Arts* (April 1978): 125–36.

Keen, Benjamin, ed. and trans. *The Life of the Admiral Christopher Columbus by His Son Ferdinand.* New Brunswick, 1959.

————. *The Aztec Image in Western Thought.* New Brunswick, 1971.

Laudonnière, René Goulaine de. *L'histoire notable de la Floride*. Paris, 1586. We have used the Kraus Reprint (Nendeln, Liechstenstein: Bibliothèque Elzevirienne, 1972), vol. 74, of the Paris, 1853, edition. English trans. *Three Voyages*, with notes and introduction by Charles E. Bennett. Gainesville, 1975.

Léry, Jean de. *Histoire d'un voyage fait en la terre du Brésil, autrement dite Amerique*. La Rochelle, 1578; Geneva, 1585; Lausanne, 1972. English trans. *History of a Voyage to the Land of Brazil, Otherwise Called America* by Janet Whatley. Berkeley, 1990.

Lestringant, Frank. "André Thevet (1504–92)." In *Publications de l'Académie des Sciences d'Outre-mer. Travaux et Mémoires: Hommes et Destins. (Dictionnaire Biographique d'Outre-mer)* 4 (Paris, n.d.): 668–71.

———. *André Thevet, cosmographe des derniers Valois* (Geneva, 1991).

———. "La conférence de Saint-Malo (1552–1553)." In *La Renaissance et le Nouveau Monde*, ed. Alain Parent et al., 37–44. Quebec, 1984.

———. "La conférence de Saint-Malo, aujourd'hui." *Etudes Canadiennes/Canadian Studies* 17 (1984): 53–68.

———. "Fictions de l'espace brésilien à la Renaissance: l'example de Guanabara." In *Arts et légendes d'espaces: figures du voyage et rhétoriques du monde*, ed. F. Lestringant and Christian Jacob, 205–56. Paris, 1981.

———. "The Myth of the Indian Monarchy: An Aspect of the Controversy between Thevet and Léry (1575–1585)." In *Indians and Europe: An Interdisciplinary Collection of Essays*, ed. C. F. Feest, 37–60. Aachen, 1987.

———. "Notes complémentaries sur les séquelles littéraires de la Floride Française." *Bibliothèque d'Humanisme et Renaissance* 45 (1983): 331–41.

———. "Nouvelle-France et fiction cosmographique dans l'oeuvre d'André Thevet." *Etudes Littéraires* (April—Aug. 1977): 145–73.

———. "Les représentations du sauvage dans l'iconographie relative aux ouvrages du cosmographe André Thevet." *Bibliothèque d'Humanisme et Renaissance* 40 (1978): 583–95.

———. "Les sequelles littéraires de la Floride Française: Laudonnière, Hakluyt, Thevet, Chauveton." *Bibliothèque d'Humanisme et Renaissance* 44 (1982): 7–36.

———. "La ville d'Angoulême et ses métamorphoses dans l'oeuvre du cosmographe André Thevet (1504–1592)." *Société Archéologique et Historique de la Charente. Extrait des mémoires* (1977–78): 29–50.

Levillier, Roberto. *Américo Vespucio. El Neuvo Mundo. Cartas relativas a sus viajes y descubrimientos.* Buenos Aires, 1951.

Lussagnet, Suzanne. *Les Français en Amérique pendant la deuxième moitié du xvie siècle: Le Brésil et les Brésiliens par André Thevet.* Introduction by C.-A. Julien. Paris, 1953.

Métraux, Alfred. "Un chapitre inédit du cosmographe André Thevet sur la géographie et l'ethnographie du Brésil." *Journal de la Société des Américanistes* 25 (1933): 31–40.

Morison, Samuel Eliot. *Admiral of the Ocean Sea: A Life of Christopher Columbus.* 2 vols. Boston, 1942.

———. *The European Discovery of America: The Southern Voyages A.D. 1492–1616.* New York, 1974.

Pagden, A. R., ed. and trans. *Hernán Cortés: Letters from Mexico.* New York, 1971.

Pinto, Estevão. "O Franciscano André Thevet." *Cultura Política* 3 (1943): 118–36.

Prescott, William H. *The History of The Conquest of Peru*, ed. J. F. Kirk. 2 vols. Philadelphia, 1874.

Prestage, Edgar. *Afonso de Albuquerque, Governor of India.* Watford, 1929.

Purchas, Samuel. *Hakluytus posthumus, or, Purchas his pilgrimes.* 5 vols. London, 1624–26; 20 vols. Glasgow, 1905–7.

Ramusio, Giovanni Battista. *Primo volume delle navigationi et viaggi.* Venice, 1550. We have used the Venice, 1606 edition.

———. *Terzo volume delle navigationi et viaggi.* Venice, 1556. We have used the Venice, 1606 edition.

Reverdin, Olivier. *Quatorze Calvinistes chez les Topinambous: Histoire d'une mission genevoise au Brésil (1556–1558).* Geneva, 1957.

Roy, Jean-L. "Un Français au Brésil au xvie siècle: André Thevet cosmographe." *Revue d'Histoire de l'Amérique Française* 21 (1967): 363–96.

Salwen, Bert. "The Reliability of André Thevet's New England Material." *Ethnohistory* 10 (1963): 183–85.

Sanceau, Elaine. *Indies Adventure: The Amazing Career of Afonso de Albuquerque*. London, 1936.

Schlesinger, Roger, ed., and Arthur P. Stabler, trans. *André Thevet's North America: A Sixteenth-Century View*. Kingston, 1986.

Silveira Cardozo, Manoel da. "Some Remarks Concerning André Thevet." *The Americas* 1 (1944): 15–36.

Skelton, R. A., ed. and trans. *Magellan's Voyage: A Narrative Account of the First Circumnavigation.*, 2 vols. New Haven, 1969.

Staden, Hans. *Warhaftig Historia und Beschreibung eyner Landtschafft der wilden, nacketen, grimmigen menschfresser Leuthen in der Newenwelt America gelegen. . . .* Marpurg, 1557. English trans. Malcolm Letts: *Hans Staden: The True History of His Captivity, 1557*. New York, 1929.

Sturtevant, William C. "First Visual Images of Native America." In *First Images of America: The Impact of the New World on the Old*, ed. F. Chiappelli. 2 vols. Berkeley, 1976. 1:417–54.

Thacher, John B. *Christopher Columbus: His Life, His Work, His Remains*. 3 vols. New York, 1903–4.

Thevet, André. *Cosmographie de Levant*. Lyon, 1554; Lyon and Antwerp, 1556.

———. *La cosmographie universelle*. 2 vols. Paris, 1575.

———. *Les singularitez de la France Antarctique, autrement nommée Amerique*. Paris, 1557; Paris and Antwerp, 1558.

———. *Les vrais pourtraits et vies des hommes illustres, Grez, Latins, et payens receuilliz de leurs tableaux, livres, medailles antiques et modernes*. 2 vols. Paris, 1584. Reprint Delmar, N.Y., 1973.

Touzard, Daniel. "André Thevet d'Angoulesme: Géographe et historien, introducteur du tabac en France (1504–1592)." *Bulletin et Mémoires de la Société Archéologique et Historique de la Charente*, 7th ser. 7 (1907–8): 1–47.

Whatley, Janet. "Savage Hierarchies: French Catholic Observers of the New World." *Sixteenth Century Journal* 17 (1986): 319–30.

# Index